Love & Light

December 29, 2023

Sharon Wagner

A DIVINE INTERVENTION
Revelations about Life and Death

SHARON WAGNER

Library of Congress Txu002195236

Book cover and interior design by BookBaby

BookBaby Publishing

ISBN: 978-1-66786-254-5 (print)
ISBN: 978-1-66786-255-2 (eBook)

ACKNOWLEDGMENTS

My heartfelt thanks go to many friends who have listened and supported my efforts for almost twenty years leading up to this momentous occasion. Writing this book has been a labor of Love. Publishing this book is a leap of Faith believing that the knowledge revealed may give others a better understanding of the unseen world we are connected to, how things work, and why things are the way they are.

Special thanks go to Paul Jensen who did the hardest initial editing and encouraged me to better explain and clarify the experiences, feelings, knowledge, and understandings. Also, to Paul's wife and friend, Barbara, who supported him as he used his valuable time to do this for me. To Peri Miller, who did the final editing, and gave me invaluable suggestions and support. I could not have accomplished this without her. Also to Patty MacKay for expert computer skills at the last minute. To Christy Whitman, her staff, and her book, *The Desire Factor,* which inspired me to follow my dream. To Christel Hughes and her staff of The Academy of the Soul for their ongoing support.

Last, but not least, to BookBaby Publishing and their entire staff.

DEDICATION

One of my Divine guides came to me years ago and brought me to the Other Side. He showed me a higher dimensional earth and answered a multitude of questions.

His mission was to give me information to increase my knowledge and understanding so that I might reconsider plans to end my life. He never told me his name or the names of those who sent him. He referred to them as 'They' and the 'Others'. After writing down this knowledge, I came to believe that it was an extraordinary Divine Intervention.

With love and appreciation, this book is dedicated to the Divine Being that brought me to the Other Side, and also to 'They' and the 'Others' for intervening in my life. I also dedicate this book to the six teachers/guides that graciously answered more of my questions and explained each in great detail.

Every day that I enjoy life on this beautiful planet, I realize it is an honor and privilege to be here. I am forever grateful to God, 'Them', and my unseen Divine friends who have been my constant companions guiding and supporting me all my life. Without their assistance, this book would not exist.

A DIVINE INTERVENTION
Revelations about Life and Death

PART TWO

INTRODUCTION

This book is about an extraordinary spiritual experience that happened years ago during my first semester of college. Seeing and feeling struggles and hardships of life bothered me even at a young age, and could see no reason to live. After secretly planning my suicide at nineteen, everything was thought out except the timing. One night, I was having second thoughts about ending my life and wished there was someone to talk with since I had not confided in anyone. Thankfully, sleep took over and ended my anxiety.

During the night, a spiritual being visited me, who I thought was one of my spirit guides. He knew all about my life, my plan, and my past lives! He took me to the Other Side, showed me an earlier past life, showed me Earth in a different dimension, and answered a multitude of questions. While writing this information down, I realized that this had been an extraordinary Divine Intervention.

In 2003, I had more questions and had another Divine Intervention on the Other Side with more teachers/guides. Both experiences occurred in what I call the dream-state of mind, but were so vivid, it felt like it really happened.

My original intervention was life changing, but I told no one about it for two years. A search of science and the world's significant religions finally convinced me that what my spirit guide told me was the truth, and I could then speak about it. However, very few people have heard this story until now.

There are two sections in this book. Part One contains the timeless wisdom revealed about life and death in both the Physical and Spirit Realms. Part Two contains eighteen personal stories that I feel confirm the information revealed in Part One.

The intention of writing this book is to share these revelations. This knowledge can help improve and inspire the lives of those searching for answers about life and death in the Physical and Spirit Realms. It can help reduce one's fear of death, help people realize how powerful they are, and how influential they may become. Especially, this wisdom can help increase conscious awareness on all levels and aspects of life.

The mind is impressive, with unlimited abilities. The physical body is a medical miracle, sending subtle signals to help keep us well. This book is about the deep connection of the soul within the heart, the Divine essence of God. This connection allows us to open our hearts, live out of love rather than fear, and understand the importance of learning life lessons while still living in the Physical Realm.

Once we apply the wisdom from the lessons learned and change behaviors, it becomes possible to create the life of our dreams, our personal Heaven on Earth.

PART ONE

*Revelations about Life and Death
in the Physical and Spirit Realms*

CHAPTER 1

My Almost Suicide

Have you ever felt such despair that you asked yourself, "Who am I, and why am I here?" Have you ever had a dream so vivid you questioned whether it was real? Could you see, feel, smell, hear, and talk with people you have never seen before in places you have never been? Did a dream experience ever affect your life or answer mystical questions you were asking? Could you see your life from a different, higher, broader perspective? Has a dream altered your attitude, thoughts, beliefs, and ultimately, your actions?

Each of these things happened to me many years ago! Every aspect of life - my thoughts, beliefs, and plans - changed that night, and those changes are still affecting me.

While I grew up in a typical middle-class household of the 1950s and 1960s, my life appeared normal to friends and neighbors. At nineteen, my spiritual connection was causing me to think differently and to ask questions. One night in my first semester of college, I had an extraordinary spiritual experience that changed my life forever! However, it seemed to be a beautiful, vividly detailed dream. As I tried to write it down, I realized the importance of it. I also realized that no words can adequately describe the breathtakingly beautiful sights, the vivid colors, the majestic music, and the resulting emotions felt in my heart and deep within my soul. It still feels as though it happened just last week.

Now, years later, knowing what I know now and seeing my life from a more objective and broader perspective, I realize my dream experience was more of a spiritual Divine Intervention. After this dream experience, I investigated science and the major religions for two years. I learned different scientific and religious facts, doctrines, and beliefs, and finally accepted that the information given in the dream-state was truth. The information was also consistent with my personal spiritual experiences and beliefs. It was not until then that I could freely discuss this life-changing experience.

The information given during this dream, though, contradicted what I had learned growing up. It was the late 1960s and no one that I was aware of - college students, adults, and clergy - spoke of these kinds of things. I believed that everyone would think there was something wrong with me, or that I had had a nervous breakdown, or needed psychological counseling. Most of all, I convinced myself that no one would believe me.

I realize now that I have always been an empathetic person, able to feel the emotions of others. At that time, my feelings were profound, but were rarely my own. When I looked at someone, I could feel the pain in his or her heart. I also felt the sadness, fear, doubt, despair, disappointments, and heartaches of people that I knew, or read about, or even heard about on the nightly news. The sense of shock, anger, inconsolable grief, and utter loss at the death of a loved one was the worst. When I was younger and first heard the song, *Puff the Magic Dragon*, tears welled up, and I cried at the end of the song for the poor dragon, who was lonely after his best friend grew up and no longer played with him! Thankfully, I can laugh about it now, even though I still feel the sadness of it.

My idealistic nature was confused, but I was realistic enough to figure out that life is all about change, that positive change is possible, is sometimes necessary, and could be a good thing. However, I also saw that change was traumatic for most people, and that happiness, peace, love, and joy were rarely felt by the majority of those I saw. This did not give me much to look forward to in my life.

Let me give you a little background before telling of that memorable night. My younger life had been normal. A couple of my closest friends thought that I had it better than most kids my age. I had fun year-round: swimming in the summer, playing outdoor games with neighborhood kids in the fall, ice skating in the winter, and riding my bicycle in the spring. My father worked full time, while my mother was at home taking care of the household, my older brother, and myself.

Watching and listening to people had become my favorite pastime. It seemed like people mostly talked about everything that was wrong in their lives. The enjoyable things and personal accomplishments were mentioned only as afterthoughts. People's expectations were rarely satisfied, causing disappointment and heartache. People disagreed with each other and often were unwilling to consider each other's perspective. Compromise leading to the best outcome for all was rare. One or two people working together on a project believed, "It's my way or no way at all," and then wondered why others got angry.

At twelve, I had tried to run away from home, falsely believing that I was adopted and did not belong in my family because I rarely felt the same as they did about anything. However, my mother assured me I belonged in the family and eventually, I accepted that it was true.

As I grew older and watched adults, I became increasingly consumed with doubt and despair about life. My father continued working full time and was usually tired. While at home, he occupied his time with solving problems and fixing things around the house. My mother suffered from three life-threatening health conditions for years, so my brother and I helped around the house when we could.

During my early teen years, family members and friends lost their jobs, or worse. One of our neighbors had to deal with devastating health conditions. Death left single mothers with young children, resulting in heartache, loss, grief, misery, and constant struggle. Gossiping was a favorite past time, along with voicing their distrust, judgment, and criticism of others. Hypocrisy and double standards ran rampant. People would say one thing and then do the opposite. This seemed to occur often, and not just in my narrowly focused world. None of this seemed acceptable to my personal sense of moral judgment, integrity, and loyalty. This also made me question the meaning of life.

As I passed through those emotional teenage years and approached college and adulthood, I realized I did not want any part of working hard all day, having an unhappy personal life, and feeling miserable. There were more questions than answers. "Why is there so much pain, misery, and struggle for so many people in the world? Why are things the way they are? What is the point of our lives, or even of humanity as a whole? Why are we here on planet Earth?" Finally, "What is the real Truth?" Not the different versions of theologians everywhere, but "What is God's real Truth?" I had learned about Heaven, the angels, Jesus, and God and wanted to go Home where I knew everything was perfect. My only way out was to take my own life, and I began planning my exit.

High School had its good times and bad, but mostly good. Graduation passed. I enrolled in my first semester of college and had a roommate who I knew from high school. We successfully compromised on all the concerns of our tiny, shared room. Classes started, the work piled up, and studying occupied most of our time.

One thing that I never shared with anyone was that I had meticulously planned my suicide weeks before college began - all except for the final timing. The semester was still young. I was getting used to this new learning format, meeting new people, and being away from home, which I had looked forward to.

Because my mother had been ill for so long, I needed to go home on weekends to shop and cook for the week, clean the house, and then get back to school. The Vietnam War was raging, and they had drafted my brother into the Army. My father took care of everything else during the week. It was always busy.

I have finally realized that life's journey is different for each person. We each have unique gifts to contribute to the whole, but also have individual traumas and difficulties to overcome. We must learn to make peace with and face these difficulties with compassion, love, and forgiveness for ourselves and for everyone else on their own life journey. Embracing the wisdom that results can change thoughts and beliefs, leading to better and happier outcomes.

Imagine that one person within a family or community or country is one piece of a vast puzzle. Each piece is unique within the whole and necessary to complete the puzzle. Each person never realizes how the other pieces appear, where their own location is within the whole, how they are individually contributing, or how important they are to the whole, even to humanity. Are you a corner piece? Are you the critical last piece to complete the puzzle? All pieces are important and influence the other surrounding pieces no matter where they are.

As I remember that magical night of my Divine Intervention, over forty years have passed. Few people have heard about my life-changing experience until now. However, I feel compelled to share this wisdom, hoping to answer questions that others may have along the winding path of life's journey.

Hopefully, this true story will help open hearts and touch souls. We have awareness about our mind and physical body, but not as much about our soul. This knowledge may help to answer various mystical questions about different aspects of life and death from a higher, broader perspective, or at least help one consider the possibility that not all things are what they appear to be. I especially hope this helps each person reading this story find a deep connection to their soul and to the Divine presence of God within their heart. Once this occurs, each person may feel their connection to all people, to all life on Earth, to life within the Universe, and within all time-space realities and dimensions.

Enjoy the journey!

My Divine Intervention
The Wake-up Call for My Lifelong Spiritual Journey!

It was the late 1960s, and I was in the first semester of my first year of college. It should have been the happiest time of my life. Instead, my inner thoughts were about ending my life here on Earth. The weirdest thing was that nothing was wrong with me, physically or mentally. The problem was my emotional self and the fact that I always saw and felt the negative side of life, despite the experiences and fun things to enjoy.

Now at college, my little world consumed me, giving no thought to the consequences my suicide would bring to my family and friends. No one knew my deep-down feelings, and I did not want to tell anyone either. To me, there was no way anyone would, or could, understand.

Reflecting on my emotional state of mind all those years ago, I realize how selfish, immature, and single-minded that decision was. Because of the dream-state experience of my intervention, I never have and would never again give suicide a second thought. Life is a precious gift to embrace, explore, and love. It is also rewarding to be of service to others, and to enjoy each moment we are blessed and privileged to experience the beauty of Mother Earth.

That fateful night, going to sleep was challenging while thinking about leaving this world of pain, struggle, disillusionment, disappointment, and heartache. Everything was planned - except the timing of my exit. My mind wandered, and I had second thoughts about my mother and not knowing anyone else who could help. I wished I had someone to talk with about my decision, since there was so much to consider, and my inner conflict was getting worse. At last, I was comfortable and fell asleep.

During the night, I wasn't sure if I was dreaming or awake. Lying on the bed, I turned my head to the side and saw a short, three or four foot high, normal-looking man in a dark suit, white shirt, and black tie standing next to my bed looking at me. He softly and calmly started speaking to me about my deep emotions and thoughts of suicide! I was astonished and shocked to hear him speak of these things, since I had never spoken about them to anyone. The oddest thing about this was that I had no fear of him and was not upset that he was there in my dorm room next to me. This little man never said who he was or where he came from, but he knew all about me, my idealistic feelings, dreams, disappointments, plans, and past lives!

My new friend continued: "There is a group of beings who feel your suicide would be detrimental to your soul's development. This lifetime is significant for you, since you will take care of many people. You took your own life long ago, and it has taken many lifetimes - forty-two, to be exact - for you to have reached the level of spiritual knowledge you have obtained up to this point."

Reincarnation was never a belief taught in school. Even though I was vaguely aware of reincarnation from discussions of other religions, the little man's comments seemed bizarre. The concept was familiar, but I had never investigated reincarnation or thought seriously about it. Curious, though, I asked, "Will you tell me about the previous life in which I committed suicide?"

My new friend put out his arm and offered his hand. "Take my hand. Do not be afraid. I will show you."

I did that without hesitation, and almost at once, we were both standing in the living room of a vivid, real-life home in a prior unknown time. It could have been a television or movie scene of an early western settlement home, much like the TV show "Little House on the Prairie."

A young woman sat alone at a large round wooden table with an oil lamp in the center. She was holding in her shaking hands and intently examining an old-fashioned pistol, a Colt 45. This woman was deep in thought, with a look of complete despair on her face. The time seemed long ago from the style of her hair and her long-sleeved, floor-length dress. She was in a small living room in front of a large window with curtains on each side. There was an enormous fireplace opposite the table, and a large wooden beam above that spanned the entire wall. Stairs went up along the far wall. The plain furniture was sparse but of high quality, obviously built by a talented artisan craftsman. Everything looked clean and orderly.

As I saw this young woman, I realized that she was me in a past life! She looked similar to how I look in this lifetime, yet different. I also felt an eerie, inner knowing that my new short male friend was telling me the truth! Thankfully, he spared me from watching the woman pull the trigger.

Suddenly, a new scene appeared. We were in the same living room but with people present. Two or three women were crying. Others were huddled next to the stairway, looking down at something. No one could see us or was aware that we were even present in the same room.

"What is happening now?" I asked.

Almost at once, and again like magic, we were halfway up the stairs looking down. I gasped for air when I saw the body of the young woman laid out in an open casket, looking peaceful at last. She had a new dress on and looked pretty. In my younger current life, it was customary practice to pay respects to deceased loved ones and their families in their homes, not in a funeral parlor. Therefore, this scene did not surprise me and felt that it was normal during that time period.

However, seeing myself dead in a casket so many lifetimes ago threw me into shock. I was distraught and thought, "How can this be? How can I live in this lifetime if I had taken my life in a different lifetime way back then?" According to my upbringing, you only had one life to live and could be damned to Hell for all eternity for ending your own life. The look on my face must have been a remarkable sight.

My short, new friend looked at me with loving and forgiving eyes. He calmly said, "I want to show you something else. Take my hand once again."

The next scene in the dream was astonishing. We were flying through outer space. We were amid the dark sky surrounded by millions of beautiful, bright stars. There was absolutely no sense of time or location. It was impossible to tell how long we were flying or in what direction we were traveling.

Suddenly, we came to a complete stop in mid-air. My little man waved his hand again. "Now, look below."

This unexpected sight took my breath away. There was an entire planet far beneath us. It looked just like Earth to me - the blue marble that we now see in pictures from the moon. Shortly after that, my emotions filled with peace, love, and pure joy. But to the core of my soul, I felt Unconditional Love permeating everywhere and in everything. Instead of breathing in oxygen, I breathed in Unconditional Love. There was no negativity. There are no words to adequately describe the majestic sight before me or the multitude of blissful feelings filling my entire being.

Finally, I asked, "Did I die in my sleep without knowing it? Have you come to bring me here? Is this Heaven?"

He smiled a gentle, loving, non-judgmental smile while holding back a little laugh and began his explanation. "No. That is still your decision to make. We cannot interfere with free will or choice. However, we can give you information when asked on a conscious, subconscious, or super-conscious level. That is why I am here. Before falling asleep while contemplating your decision, you wished for someone to talk to, and you had questions. This meeting is a result of your wish.

"As I told you earlier, this is a meaningful life for you, and 'They' did not want you to make the same mistake again. 'They' hope this information will answer your questions. 'They' also hope to expand your awareness and consciousness of the body, mind, and soul along with the purpose and meaning of life and death."

Moments later, after regaining my composure, I asked, "Where are we?"

My friend lovingly smiled. "We are in a higher vibrational dimension than the physical third-dimensional world that you are familiar with - similar to but different from the dream-state. This planet is a parallel world like Earth, where the souls of most people go to when they make their transition back to Spirit. It is the first of seven levels within the Spirit Realm, and each level has many purposes."

He waved his hand again. The surface of this other Earth suddenly became much closer, even though we did not seem to move. I wondered if he had moved the planet closer to us. It looked exactly like Earth. We were still above this other planet, but it was easy to see people in buildings busy working, children playing, and adults relaxing. It was just as you would expect to see on our Earth - except every person was happy! People were working for the sheer joy of it. People were in libraries, museums, and colleges continuing their education or doing whatever they loved to do for the benefit of themselves and others.

He continued, "Many people might think of this place as a perfect utopia where people live, work, and play according to their preferences while helping themselves and others advance their knowledge, understanding, and awareness of many things simultaneously. There is only Unconditional Love here."

The flood of pleasant emotions continued. It did not take long to realize that negative emotions did not exist, not even a hint of anger, jealousy, greed, or any other negative feeling, only Unconditional Love. It was sheer bliss!

After an unknown amount of time, my new friend had explained much more about this level of the Spirit Realm, our souls, and about the energy and purpose of our souls. He continued explaining the Physical Realm, the energy and nature of people, the meaning of various aspects of life, and the transition of physical life to Spirit.

When he finished, I asked, "Can I stay here? I don't want to go back."

My new short male friend smiled and, this time, laughed a little. He denied my wish. "No, you cannot stay here. You are to take care of many people. Remember? It is not your scheduled time to leave the physical world. We may not influence free will and choice. 'They' all hope that you will feel differently now and choose a different path. However, you still have free will to make your choice."

"What is going to happen to me in the future?"

He smiled again with great compassion. "We may not tell you anything about your future. That is up to you and your free will choices."

Then, I woke up! It was morning, and I was lying on my bed at college. The "dream" felt so real to me I was shocked to be back on Earth and in my body. For a short while, I was shaking all over, but knew that I had to force myself to get up, go to classes, and continue with my routine physical life as though nothing had happened. I did not dare tell anyone about this bizarre "dream".

After thinking about all the information my short new friend had conveyed to me, I realized that everything had changed! Now I could see things from a much higher, broader perspective. My physical life is the illusion - a paradox where truth is hidden in plain view. I wanted to ask him more questions, but somehow knew I would have to wait years to do that.

My eyes, ears, heart, and soul were suddenly wide open to new thoughts, beliefs, and concepts. I would never look at life the same way again. What I experienced was real to me, and no one will ever change that. Since then, I have had many spiritual experiences; some were profound, but most have been small, subtle insights whenever I asked a question or needed an explanation. I am now convinced that there are many levels of existence within many dimensions and alternate realities, all within the Force of God, or Source Energy, and also follow the Cosmic Laws of the Universe, and the Laws of Nature - and believe it or not, all without the use of drugs!

Over forty years have passed. Life continued. Some aspects were good and some were not so good. I learned lessons with each large or small experience. A new higher perspective would appear as a unique viewpoint of life opening to a greater understanding of people, patterns, thoughts, beliefs, habits, cultures, traditions, changes, and choices.

Conscious awareness increases knowledge. Knowledge increases understanding. Understanding increases wisdom. Wisdom increases the ability to change your mind, change your beliefs, and change your perspectives - all of which change your life. It is always amazing how much more I become aware of every day. One motto I have adopted is, "We don't know what we don't know!" but I am usually eager to find out more and have new experiences. My goal is to nurture the fire of passion, to love and respect each form of life. Each is a beautiful creation of God along with the Unity and Oneness of consciousness in all time-space realities and dimensions.

CHAPTER 2

Jacob

My new short cosmic friend, the teacher/guide of my Divine Intervention, never told me his name. He said that it was his essence that I would remember, which is his soul energy and vibrational frequency. He said that I could call him by any name that resonated with me. Since then, I have named him Jacob, have seen him in my dream-state, and now consider him one of my spirit guides.

In the dream-state now, he looks completely different. Instead of being a short man in a black suit, I see Jacob as a stately, distinguished-looking older man. He has shoulder-length chestnut brown hair, a short chestnut brown beard, and has beautiful cobalt blue eyes. He wears a white linen robe with a rope tied around his waist and comfortable-looking sandals. However, his appearance may look different to each person he appears to in order to help them without discomfort or fear.

The first time I met Jacob, we were in a higher-dimensional world, looking down from outer space at what appeared to be the blue marble planet. The second time, we were outside of his home, seated on a comfortable wooden bench in a gorgeous garden. Several towering trees, large flowering shrubs, and many beautiful flowers that I had never seen before surrounded the garden. The vivid colors were amazing. There was also a large, elegantly carved white stone water fountain on one side. Birds were darting from one tree to another, and I could hear their faint chirping. It was very peaceful and relaxing.

Jacob told me I would meet five other teachers/guides later. The essence of each is different, and all of them exist within the Spirit Realm. Each would talk about a different aspect of the Physical and/or Spirit Realm. Jacob also told me that none of this information is associated with any religion, culture, or tradition. He said that all people in all circumstances are equal in the eyes of God; are free, sovereign beings; and loved unconditionally by God, Source Energy.

Jacob never told me who "They" or the "Others" were that wanted me to have the intervention to receive this information. I have my suspicions, but do not know for sure and am not willing to speculate. I am grateful that they intervened on my behalf and appreciate them every day of my life.

My fear of death and my fear of the unknown have now completely disappeared. When it is time for my transition from my physical body to go back to Spirit, I know I will experience the blissful emotions that I felt at nineteen. I will gladly breathe in and absorb the unforgettable, peaceful, and comforting feelings of pure Divine Unconditional Love.

There are names for the all-encompassing higher energies that I felt that night. Source Energy, Universal Force, Great Spirit, the Divine, God, and 'ALL That Is' are several names for those energies. Since then, I have been told that there are over seventy different names for God. My belief is that these higher Divine energies are all the same energies that permeate everything, everyone, everywhere. The names most used in this book are Source Energy, God, or the Divine when referring to those energies.

Everyone has a unique personal relationship with God, which needs to be nurtured with focus and intention. When the heart is open, you may feel soul level, deep emotions, and begin to ask questions. Who am I? Why am I here on Earth? What is the meaning of life? What is the purpose of life? Why are things the way they are?

These are mystical questions. The information given to me while in the Spirit Realm will, hopefully, answer these questions. While writing and rewriting this book for the past fifteen years, I have received further information. Each time I sought clarification or asked a question, I would receive a mental vision, an inspiration, hear an explanation, or see a concept which explained what I needed to understand to increase my knowledge, resulting in greater insights and profound wisdom.

Jacob: Energy, Life, and Transformation

Jacob smiled at me and took a deep breath. I felt calm and at peace, enjoying the gorgeous array of colors in the beautiful garden we were sitting in. He finally said, "You have more questions about life and death, including how and why are things the way they are. We are here to help answer those questions. Ready?"

"Yes, of course! I am looking forward to hearing about everything."

"Good, let us begin! It is a scientific fact that the physical body works on electrical energy. It is God, or Source Energy, which gives a gentle jolt, or spark, of electrical energy to the heart of a developing fetus, starting the heart to beat while still in the mother's womb. Electrical instruments can detect when this happens and can also monitor the electrical beats of the unborn fetus for any abnormalities while still in the womb. If all goes well during a pregnancy, the physical body of the baby goes through the birthing process and life begins in the physical world after the baby has taken its first breath of air.

"The soul is separate from the body, though. It can enter the physical body any time after the heart starts beating. The soul becomes an internal aspect of the Divine for the physical body's entire life, existing at the soul's unique vibrational frequency. Each physical body, from that point onward, becomes an individual source of electrical energy and receives and sends out power on its own unique wavelength, or vibrational frequency, while the heart is still beating. This is true of all physical bodies: men, women, and children from every corner of the world. It makes no difference where they live, what they believe, what their appearance or social status is, or how much money or power they have. Concerning this, all of humankind is equal."

"One example of this continuous presence of electrical energy," Jacob continued, "is the nerve synapses found in your mind. The brain's electrical nerve impulses transmit from one neuron to another. This occurs each time a nerve cell transmits thought patterns and feelings, such as pain, love, or fear, to and from the brain. Electrical instruments can also detect these for any abnormalities.

"The most notable example of this is the function of the heart, where the electrical spark of Source Energy originates. Monitored electrical impulses detect abnormalities within all areas of the heart. The presence or absence of these abnormal impulses determines the presence or absence of the life force energy of the physical body.

"As you may already be aware, the heart is sometimes electrically shocked to restart the beating of it. If the restart is unsuccessful, the electrical impulses are no longer detected, the life force of the body ceases, and the body dies. The electrical energy—our original spark of life - is the connection to our soul energy, which does not die and is still intact. The soul energy transforms and moves to a higher frequency, or dimension, where it is invisible in the Physical Realm. There is no death. There is only a change in vibrational frequency, or dimension.

"When people 'die,' the soul energy remains. Each person was in Spirit before being born into the Physical Realm. You are a spiritual being, having a temporary human experience. The Spirit Realm is the home of the soul."

Jacob paused a minute before resuming. "Here is a short comparison, but with a broader perspective to think about. Different detectable energies exist at different frequencies within the Universe. The wavelengths of visible light in the Physical Realm are few compared to the full spectrum of other possibilities, such as gamma rays, X-rays, ultraviolet light, laser light rays, microwaves, and sound, ultrasound, and radio waves. However, these wavelengths are not visible. We need specialized instruments to detect and measure them. Each wavelength of energy, though, has its own unique qualities, benefits, purposes, and importance.

"In principle, it is the same for human beings. Each person is like a different wavelength of energy. All physical bodies have much in common. However, the soul of each person is invisible, exists at a unique vibrational frequency, and has its own unique qualities, benefits, purpose, and importance."

Jacob smiled again and asked, "Do you have questions?"

"No. This was never taught to me, but it all makes sense. You've just answered several questions that I've been wondering about for a long time! Thank you, Jacob. Please continue."

Jacob: Radio Stations

"Okay, I will continue. Let us explore and compare how the energy system of a physical body functions by comparing it to a radio station, with which I am sure you are familiar with.

"The vibrational frequency of a person is comparable to the frequency modulation of radio waves. There are AM (amplitude modulation), FM (frequency modulation), VHF (very high frequency), and UHF (ultra-high frequency). Many radio stations use the two most common frequency ranges, AM, and FM. Each station is a power source that transmits its signal and programing at a unique wavelength, or frequency, staying unique and independent of other stations. You need to change the dial, or frequency, to find different stations.

"Each person is a unique source of power, always conducting, transmitting, and receiving energy. The physical body is like the radio station, while the personality, or soul energy, compares to the station's programming. All people everywhere have physical, emotional, and spiritual things in common. The personality, or programming, of each person is unique and independent, with specific qualities, characteristics, and importance. However, the personality and emotions of empathic people may react differently due to their sensitivity to the energies of high or low vibrational frequencies. One crucial fact is that you can listen to only one radio station at a time. Other stations are broadcasting, but you have to move the dial, the frequency, to hear them."

"The same is true when the spark of life leaves the physical body. The soul energy automatically transforms back to a higher frequency, where it is no longer detected, seen, or easily accessed from the Physical Realm. Nothing changes except the frequency at which the person's soul energy is transmitting.

"Souls in the Spirit Realm are at various higher frequencies, depending on the level where they live. When souls live on the same higher frequency, they can see each other as clearly as you see each other on Earth. However, those in the Physical Realm who have learned to access these higher soul frequencies may see, hear, and sometimes smell the soul essence of someone in spirit."

"Another essential fact involves the quality and power of the radio signal. The range and clarity of the transmission depend on the amount of energy available. The ability to receive these signals depends on the strength of the antenna and the amount of power within the receiver. Sound waves release and move out in a circular pattern. The closer to the source, or radio station, the louder and stronger is the signal. The higher its power, the farther out the signal can travel and still be received. However, the farther away it travels from the source, the weaker and more jumbled the transmission becomes as it overlaps with other frequencies, making it difficult to distinguish each station.

"The same is true for human beings. The farther away we are from God, our Source Energy, the weaker the connection to the love and peace in one's soul. Energies become jumbled, overlapping with other energies, causing confusion, doubt, despair, depression, fear, and anxiety."

"Throughout life, each person has free will and must make many choices. A person learns lessons by listening, observing, and experiencing life in order to gain knowledge, understanding, and eventually, wisdom. Struggles and hardships also teach us many lessons.

"One may learn lessons alone, within a group of people, or through a combination of both. A person becomes strong either way. The person experiences soul growth with each lesson learned, which helps develop the individual's personality and increases his or her happiness and power. As this increases, the ability to accomplish things, make good choices, and be responsible for one's self and others also increases.

"Awareness of the well-being of others continually changes and expands. This changes the perspectives and priorities of each individual. As people become stronger and wiser, so does their power to bring about changes in their own lives, to influence the lives of others, and to influence large groups of people. This individual growth continues until the spark of life no longer exists.

"When like-minded people gather with a specific intention or to raise the vibration of a person, place, or situation, the power produced increases exponentially based on the number of people involved. This rise in vibration is called a 'Field Effect' or 'Maharishi Effect,' and has the fantastic ability to achieve the intended desire." *I call this the "miracle zone!" Sharon*

Jacob paused before continuing. "Life can be a complex journey. Is this helping you to see the bigger picture? Is it making sense to you? Does it answer your questions?"

Mesmerized by Jacob and all he was sharing, I said, "Yes. It makes sense. The bigger picture is what I'm trying to visualize. I understand, so far. I have questions about the energies of the body, but want to wait until I hear more. Thank you."

"May God's Love, Light, Peace, Joy, and Blessings,
be with you on your journey"

~ J A C O B ~

22

CHAPTER 3

Robert: Spirit Realm, the First Level

A moment later, while listening to Jacob, I suddenly saw another man standing by the water fountain. It seemed odd I had not seen him arrive.

Jacob turned toward him with a big smile and motioned him to come forward. Jacob put his hand on the man's shoulder and said, "Let me introduce you to Robert. He lives on a higher frequency level within the Spirit Realm. Robert will explain the different energy or frequency levels that exist, supply more information about this first energy level in the Spirit Realm, and finally, clarify the transformation of soul energy between the Physical Realm and the Spirit Realm."

Robert looked distinguished, much like Jacob, since he was also wearing a long white robe with a braided rope tied around his waist and comfortable looking sandals. However, he had pure white hair and a full beard. His large, deep-set eyes were a mesmerizing bright sky-blue color. His demeanor conveyed authority and wisdom, but also patience and love.

All three of us sat on Jacob's large comfortable bench. Within a minute of silence, a sense of peace filled the air. Robert, with a smile, began speaking. "There are many levels of energy, or frequencies, within the Spirit Realm. This first level is at a higher frequency than the third-dimensional world and is called the astral world, the fourth dimension, or the psychic level. It is a world similar to the physical world in almost every detail - except time and space are not linear.

"This first level astral world supplies a temporary familiar environment to make the death experience, the transition of one's soul energy from the Physical Realm to the Spirit Realm, less traumatic. The similarity to Earth helps reduce one's fear of death, that may arise during the crossing over, or transition. After transitioning, one's soul energy remains the same. The only difference is a shift to a higher vibrational frequency within the Spirit Realm.

"As Jacob said earlier, this first frequency level gives souls time to recover, if necessary, from a painful physical or emotional lifetime. They may rest until the soul is ready to remember being in the Spirit Realm, about spiritual growth, and about the higher-frequency levels that a soul may live on while in the Spirit Realm.

"Abilities are learned and practiced here on this first level before returning to the Physical Realm. The Light here in the Spirit Realm is much brighter than in the Physical Realm. This Light may be the reason there are reports of seeing a beautiful bright white light at the end of a tunnel as one transitions.

"Each higher level is more glorious than the earlier level. This brilliant Light is due to a greater conscious awareness of God's Love, Strength, Peace, Power, Wisdom, Joy, and Perfection, which is the highest frequency of energy. Therefore, if you ever get lost within the Spirit Realm, it is always best to move toward the brightest Light that you see. Then ask for help, which is only a thought away. Stay relaxed. Then look up and around. Help will arrive soon."

Robert paused, smiled, and said, "I hope that helps explain a few things. Do you have questions?"

"No, not at this time. It's easy to understand by the way you explain things. Thank you. Although, there is much more to process than I expected."

Robert: Physical Realm, Soul Energy

Robert looked at me. "You are welcome. If you have no questions, I'll continue with more about soul energy, but in the Physical Realm. Are you ready for more?"

"Yes, by all means. This is fascinating!"

"Okay. Let us proceed. The vibrational frequency on this first level of the Spirit Realm is higher than, but is closest to, that of the Physical Realm. Each person in the Physical Realm naturally vibrates at a different vibrational frequency. Those with a higher vibration may naturally perceive this energy level, clairvoyantly see this parallel world, and may also access its flow of energy and information for healing, explanations, or solutions. If a person consciously shifts his or her vibration to this higher frequency level, he or she may also perceive the same."

"Soul energy is the spiritual essence of God within each person. Since the path to the soul is through the heart, it can be a deeply personal and emotional energy. Many people in the physical world avoid deep emotions. This avoidance inhibits or block emotional energies of the heart, and thus the connection to the soul energy. Life becomes out of balance, and there is less harmony between the body, the mind, the emotions, and the soul, or spirit.

"A person's true soul essence is spirit, the true nature of the soul. The soul energy always stays intact. However, the quality, amount, and power of the soul energy will increase or decrease depending on lessons learned while living in the Physical Realm. If one truly learns a lesson, one's behavior will change based on the wisdom gained from the lesson. If one does not learn the lesson, the pattern of circumstances will continue until it is. This occurs with each learning experience, with or without conscious awareness. Either way, knowledge, understanding, and wisdom increase once behavior changes.

"One sign that a lesson still needs to be learned is when something is said or done that continues to trigger a negative emotion and causes irrational behavior. However, this can become another opportunity for further self-examination to discover the deeper cause of this triggered reaction and to learn another deep aspect of oneself. Thoughts, beliefs, and choices change with each lesson learned. The vibrational frequency of the soul increases and transforms one's life."

"Soul energy increases whenever there are high vibrational emotions, such as peace, love, joy, compassion, forgiveness, and happiness. Low vibrational emotions, such as hatred, anger, fear, depression, and resentment, can deplete soul energy. Both types of powerful emotions have a great deal of energy. Personal choice about how to control emotions decides whether the soul energy increases or decreases.

"Doing the right thing and performing selfless acts of kindness can also increase the vibrational frequency of the soul. Being aware of one's negative feelings and overcoming the urge to act on them with self-control helps to release those negative feelings and increases one's personal power to control impulsive decisions. Both the lesson learned, and the release of negative feelings, help to allow the higher vibrational energies of Light and Love to enter the physical body, replacing those negative feelings.

"It is also possible for each person in the Physical Realm to shift his or her energy consciously to a higher vibration within his or her day-to-day life. The conscious choice to shift energy is a change of how you feel in your emotions. However, there is often conflict between the intellectual energies of the mind and the inspirational energies of the heart, or soul. Final decisions are usually best made when both the heart and the mind are in total agreement.

"One good example of this mind-versus-heart conflict is the discussion of money. Should one be responsible and pay the rent, mortgage, or car payment? Should one go on vacation instead and have a good time because of stress or depression? Another option might be to pay the bills and go on a short one- or two-day trip instead? Personal choice of behavior decides the outcome. When both the mind and heart agree, there is balance and wisdom, which helps prevent future hardships.

"Once one is aware of being in a prolonged emotional state, such as depression, sadness, or frustration, there are several things that will help change that emotional state. It is possible to consciously and objectively change one's perspective of a situation to a higher and broader viewpoint. One can list things to be grateful for, or listen to uplifting music. One can also go for a walk, spend time in Nature, watch a funny movie, or do any enjoyable activity that brings one closer to being happy and feeling the emotions of love, peace, and joy. Each time there is a shift in emotion to help one feel better, one reaches a higher consciousness level, or vibrational frequency. When that consistently occurs, one can perceive his or her life from a higher, broader perspective, making positive changes easier throughout one's life."

Robert paused and took a deep breath. He appeared to be thinking. Then he suddenly continued speaking. "Here's another thought that may help you better understand the energies of the physical body. Everyone has a body, a mind, and a soul. At all times, the corresponding physical, mental, emotional, and spiritual energies synergistically work together within and around the body. The energies around the body are invisible, etheric energies known as one's Aura. The energies within the body are electrical, with a multitude of pathways similar, in principle, to the circulatory system of the blood. There are seven major energy centers, called chakras, which are found up and down the center of the body. Each chakra regulates the flow of energy within its horizontal zone of influence and has a corresponding color associated with its energy vibration.

"If there is a physical or emotional trauma, the body absorbs and holds onto that trauma energy somewhere in the body until the person processes and releases that energy. If this release does not occur, the trauma energy remains somewhere within the body. As a result, the normal flow of energy is disrupted. If the free flow of energy is blocked for a substantial length of time, the body will reroute the energies, like going around a dam.

"However, this alternate energy flow may cause physical problems within each chakra's zone of influence, and eventually cause illness or disease. A few examples of these physical problems may affect the endocrine glands that produce hormones, such as the pituitary and thymus glands, and/or other organs such as the liver and kidneys, and/or systems such as the immune and nervous systems."

"Some people can adjust their conscious awareness and vibration to match the vibration of the chakras, the colored energy centers of the physical body and aura. By doing so, they clairvoyantly see the colors to figure out if there may be a problem. The colors of each chakra can be vibrant, dull, cloudy, clear, or even change to a different color depending on the traumas or stresses withheld in the body. The etheric bodies surrounding the physical body, collectively called the Aura, also have corresponding colors.

"These invisible etheric energies of the Aura can be felt if a person is sensitive to the energies of his or her surroundings. One example is sensing when someone silently walks up behind you. Another example is when you arrive at a party and the group's happiness is palpable upon entering the room. The same is true at a wake. One may feel deep sorrow and a sense of loss upon entering the funeral parlor. Many people instinctively feel these emotions and the subtle differences of energy, but may not be aware of why."

Robert: Physical Realm, Soul Memory

"Does this makes sense to you? Any questions or comments?"

"Yes, it does make sense. I have no questions or comments. You are answering more of my questions about life on Earth. Thank you. Please continue."

"Okay, good news. While in the Physical Realm, the soul memory of earlier lifetimes is suppressed but not erased. The soul memory may still appear in the subconscious mind in dreams, visions, as a feeling of conviction, or a knowing of something to be true or false, with no clear reason.

"Depending on the level of spiritual understanding and awareness, one's spirit, or soul memory, may bring clarity and conviction or it may cause confusion and conflict. For instance, if one is not familiar with reincarnation or doesn't believe in it, dreams or visions of unknown places, people, and experiences may bring confusion, prompting the person to wonder why these visions are occurring. If one has a strong attraction to certain foods, countries, or cultures, one's soul memory of earlier lifetimes may explain the influence and bring clarity to this attraction.

"This remembrance can also occur while sleeping and may be perceived as a dream. However, the subject is usually different from anything he or she has previously experienced. There may be exotic places, unusual people, and even different music never before heard. There may be a message that answers a question or a vision showing the solution to a problem. Also, the details may be so vivid that one might believe that the experience had really happened.

"Regular dreams usually relate to day-to-day concerns, worst fears coming true, daily frustrations, or a combination of them all. Regular dreams can also feel real, but usually can be explained and inspired by the current conditions of one's life."

"The nature of someone's personality, essence, and character while in the Physical Realm will reflect that person's unique qualities accumulated over many lifetimes. If a soul works hard to become an expert in a certain field in consecutive lifetimes, the ability remains with the soul in future lives. The choice to further perfect the ability also remains in each lifetime. An example of this is when a young child sits down at a piano and easily plays beautiful music after having only a few piano lessons. We may consider he or she a child prodigy, an expert, or expert in his or her perfected field. That lifetime is one of mastership.

"The subconscious memory of accumulated unique qualities from past lives may influence the person's likes, dislikes, and masterships in all areas of life. The soul has a predetermined purpose to return to the Physical Realm in each life-time. This purpose is unique to each person, and will often be called a burning desire, the heart's desire, the life purpose, or the reason for living. It can bring happiness, fulfillment, peace, and passion, all of which contribute to the mean-ing of one's life. Each person unknowingly searches for this purpose until he or she discovers and embraces the awareness of it. Once aware of the life purpose, one can then take action to fulfill it."

"The soul knows the purpose for which one is born in the current lifetime before the mind figures it out. The soul draws to itself situations, circumstances, and opportunities that help one realize one's purpose. Predetermined life lessons will occur in order to gain experience, knowledge, understanding, and wisdom, guiding the search for one's purpose. Each person, though, has free will to choose whether or not to take advantage of any or all growth opportunities available in the Physical Realm. One result may be a great hardship that is turned around to help others navigate the same troubles. Or, the result might be something one has a passion for and desires to share with others. Or, it may be something never expected, but that gives one a great sense of purpose and fulfillment."

Robert: Physical Realm, Just Before Death

Robert paused and looked to see if he needed to stop for questions. I shook my head and smiled. He understood and continued.

"Sometimes, upon physical death, or a short time before death occurs, a soul in Spirit will shift its energy to a lower frequency and visit the Physical Realm to assist a dying person transitioning back to the Spirit Realm. These souls may be saints, angels, Archangels, Masters, guides, deceased family members, or old friends. This visit commonly occurs to ease any fears of the dying person, to give him or her comfort, and/or to give reassurance that all is as it should be on a deeper level of consciousness.

"This visitation is why there are occasional reports in the Physical Realm of seeing angels or deceased family members or friends, especially if there was long suffering or a near-death experience. At the proper time, these spirits help with the transition. The dying person may or may not be aware of a friendly spirit until after the crossing over, or transition occurs. The assisting spirit then helps the soul of the now-deceased person shift to a higher frequency, helps him or her understand and accept what is happening, welcomes him or her home, and explains what to expect until the soul memory returns.

"Each circumstance of death is different for each person. When there is an accidental or unexpected death, the soul energy leaves the physical body of the deceased person quickly. In that case, the soul returns to spirit, but may perceive the current surroundings in the physical world for a short period. This brief delay helps to reduce the immediate trauma to the soul who transitioned. If the surroundings looked drastically different, there would be much more confusion, fear, and shock. The soul would know that something had happened but not know what, how, or why it happened, or where to find help and answers. Support comes quickly, but is best to eliminate the trauma of the situation if possible. As soon as help arrives from the Spirit Realm, the soul transitions to a higher frequency, usually to this level, and eventually learns what has happened."

Robert: Physical Realm, Soul Transition

Robert looked at me with eyebrows lifted, wondering if I was about to speak.

"I'm good. When you finish, I'll probably have questions."

With a slight smile and a compassionate look, Robert replied, "Okay. This is about the transition of the soul at the time of death of the physical body. Mostly when a soul transitions from the physical to the spirit world, the soul transports to this first level in the Spirit Realm. This fourth-dimensional level, astral world, or psychic level may appear different to each person who is transitioning depending on his or her beliefs, experiences, life circumstances, and level of conscious awareness.

"The actual transition of the soul, or transformation, is a change in vibrational frequency. It is as easy as walking through a doorway from one room to another. How this is possible is a challenge to grasp by one's limited third-dimensional mind.

"Sometimes this parallel world is so similar to the Physical Realm that newly transitioned souls may not realize that they have died. Also, occasionally, souls in spirit realize that they are deceased but don't want to leave the physical world for personal reasons. The soul stays in spirit of its own free will, but stays within the Physical Realm unable to be seen. They may go through the motions of their lives or relive a traumatic experience over and over. This situation is another reason there are sightings of spirits walking the halls, guarding something, working in the garden, or going about their daily lives. Spirits have the opportunity at any time to transition and advance to a higher frequency level. Once they realize they can do so and allow it to happen, the soul will advance to the Spirit Realm."

"Shakespeare had it right when he said, 'All the World is a stage.' There is a deeper meaning to this famous quote. While in the Physical Realm, each person plays a predetermined role that advances the growth of his or her soul. One plays a role in the Physical Realm until the 'play' ends. The transition from the physical to the spirit world is like walking off the stage and returning to the backstage area where life is real, where there are no masks, disguises, or secrets. Then, one's soul energy, or essence, returns to its higher vibrational frequency in the Spirit Realm. The energy of one's soul, figuratively, stays 'backstage,' where all future roles originate."

"The nature, or personality, of each soul stays the same as in the Physical Realm - nasty or nice, happy or sad, - until the soul energy increases through conscious awareness, knowledge, and understanding. The soul then moves to a higher frequency.

"After the transition, each soul may reunite with loved ones who already have transitioned to the Spirit Realm. Sometimes the soul needs to rest after a traumatic physical or emotional lifetime until they are ready to progress.

"After the transition, all physical limitations of the body are gone and disabilities disappear. There are no negative forces in spirit. All souls are open and honest with each other. They work together in complete balance and harmony. There is no need or want of anything. The Universal Forces of God provides all."

Robert: Spirit Realm, Soul Memory

"The complete history of the soul, including one's past lives, will ideally return slowly so as not to traumatize the person returning home. There can be many experiences and differences for each soul returning. These differences will depend on the physical, mental, and emotional circumstances of the last physical life, along with the death experience itself of the person. When there is sufficient energy, each soul - with God's Grace and Divine Love - reviews his or her earlier lifetime, sometimes referred to as the "Soul Review." During this examination, the soul objectively evaluates, without judgment or criticism, his or her predetermined purpose, or role, before reentering life in the Physical Realm.

"Also examined are one's lessons learned, and the quality of relationships to family, friends, and others. Each soul also reviews the accomplishments, failures, successes, mistakes, skills, strengths, weaknesses, and actions taken to help or hinder themselves and others. Life lessons that still need to be learned are also discussed and determined. These lessons help to increase one's capacity for love, forgiveness, compassion, cooperation, patience, joy, gratitude, humility, trust, tolerance, and understanding. Life lessons also help one overcome pride, fear, anger, jealousy, hatred, arrogance, greed, prejudice, criticism, judgment, or being too controlling. This process is quite involved.

"Before the soul plays another role in the Physical Realm, many things happen. Each soul, still living in the Spirit Realm, studies all the roles available and chooses the role that will provide the most opportunities to learn specific lessons during the next lifetime in the Physical Realm. Each soul also predetermines what abilities, handicaps, illnesses, and hardships are needed in order to better learn those lessons."

Most people on Earth, though, consider the latter as problems or obstacles instead of opportunities for soul growth! Sharon

"In order to aid the soul in learning these lessons in the next lifetime, other souls in the Spirit Realm may volunteer to play a role in his or her life, possibly the role of an antagonist, which may or may not be a wife, husband, child, in-law, or close friend. Although, when one reenters physical life, what is referred to as 'the Veil', blocks the memory of these decisions. On rare occasions, people may have dreams or visions about those who volunteered while in spirit, but will usually dismiss the meaning.

"Teachers and guides gently increase awareness and understanding of what has happened and is happening after the soul returns to spirit. Each soul learns about soul growth, about love in all its forms, and about future opportunities to aid specific spiritual growth and advance to higher frequency levels. Most importantly, each soul learns to connect with and be of service to God.

"Once the soul memory returns, the soul energy shifts to the person's earned level of consciousness and accomplishment. As the vibrational frequency increases as each soul expands and advances, the frequency level on which the soul lives also increases. The soul continues to receive knowledge and understanding from teachers and guides found on levels, or frequencies, above them. The soul also becomes a teacher/guide to souls living on levels, or frequencies, below them. While the soul is in the Spirit Realm and before returning to the Physical Realm, there is time to learn more about energy fields and how to control them, along with the principles, concepts, and different degrees of soul energy. Once the soul can learn and practice these things, one will understand why the transition between the Physical and Spirit Realms is relatively smooth.

"The teachers and guides are eager to help every soul on the path of spiritual enlightenment back to God, whether or not the person realizes that this is the journey we are all on. The destination of enlightenment and wisdom is the same for all people. There are multiple paths to reach it, but many more to distract, mislead, and tempt."

Robert stopped speaking. Before he could speak again, I said, "Wow! There is so much more to understand than expected. It all makes sense to me. This information is what I need. Thank you! What happens now?"

"Your next teacher/guide is Rebecca. Her home is in a different location. Get comfortable and relax. Close your eyes and take several deep breaths to relax and raise your vibrational frequency. Fill your heart with love. Visualize a beautiful woman waiting for you outside her villa. Visualize a beam of White

Light between yourself and Rebecca. See yourself with her standing outside in the Sun. Feel a gentle breeze on your face, relax, and keep breathing."

"May the Grace of God shower you with Blessings.
May the Love of God be with you always."

~ ROBERT ~

CHAPTER 4

Rebecca: Water, Energy, and Transformation

Robert's voice seemed to fade away to silence. Suddenly, I felt a gentle breeze on my face and opened my eyes. It shocked me to see that I was somewhere outdoors, standing in the bright sunshine, not having any idea how I could be here! Looking around, I saw a beautiful, slender, regal-looking woman with long, jet-black hair and a small crown on her head. She walked toward me and stopped about six feet away. Her smile at once put me at ease. She introduced herself but supplied no background or information about where she lives in the Spirit Realm.

"It is nice to meet you, Sharon, and I am happy you are here. The name I go by is Lady Rebecca, but please just call me Rebecca. This experience will help expand your conscious awareness of many things and, hopefully, answer some questions that have you rethinking life on Earth. My home is near here. It is a short distance behind you and just beyond the garden and trees. We can relax and be comfortable there as we talk, if you like."

"Yes, of course. That would be wonderful. I'll also enjoy seeing your beautiful garden on the way."

The garden was gorgeous. The flowers were stunning with such vibrant colors, some of which I had never seen before. We walked in silence, quietly admiring the entire area. After reaching Rebecca's one-story white stone home, we went inside to a plain, but elegant room. There were padded wooden benches along the wall and a few matching hunter-green upholstered chairs with a small wooden table beside each of them. There were several windows without glass that supplied the light.

We each sat in one of the comfortable chairs with a table between us. After another minute of silence, Rebecca smiled and spoke again. "It is my pleasure to explain and correlate the transformation of our soul energy from physical life to spirit life; to help you correlate energies of the body, mind, and soul; and also explain the application of two Universal Laws: the Law of Gravity and the Law of Cause and Effect.

"Do you remember how Jacob compared the frequency, energy, power, and programming of radio stations to the energy, power, and personality of individuals? "Similarly, I will compare the transformative qualities and properties of water to the transformation of humans from the Spirit Realm to the Physical Realm and back again after physical death.

Water is an excellent example of transformation. Exposed water evaporates as an invisible gas and eventually forms clouds. Water falls back to earth as rain, sleet, or snow. Water accumulates above and below ground in streams, lakes, and ponds, making it available to trees, plants, animals, humans, insects, and microscopic life. Dew forms on vegetation in arid climates, supplying life-saving moisture. All life requires water for survival.

"Scientifically, a water molecule is comprised of oxygen and hydrogen held together by positive and negative ions. The temperature of each molecule decides its vibration. The vibration of the molecule decides the form it takes - solid, liquid, or gas.

"The colder the molecule, the less it vibrates and the more solid it becomes. If the temperature is below freezing, 32 degrees F, the vibration is so low that water turns to a solid called ice or a semi-solid called snow or sleet. Snow can be beautiful, fun to build snowmen with, or to ski or snowshoe on. Or snow can be dangerous, with accumulations on roofs and roads. Ice is good for cooling drinks in the summer and to skate on in the winter, but it can be hazardous on any surface and may cause ice-jams on rivers.

"The warmer the molecule, the more it vibrates and transforms. If the temperature is between 32 and 212 degrees F, these molecules form a clear, colorless liquid called water. Water is one of the most precious liquids on Earth, with many benefits for humanity and all living things. It is possible to live for many days without food, but impossible to do so without water.

"If the water is boiling, or over 212 degrees F, these molecules achieve the highest vibration. As the water heats, the particles form steam, a visible vapor that rises from the boiling water and quickly disappears as an invisible gas, almost like magic. This eventually is felt as humidity in the air. Boiling water has many uses for cooking or cleaning. The moisture is welcome in hot, dry conditions, but not in tropical, wet areas.

"These three different forms of water - solid, liquid, and gas - are all composed of the same molecule made of oxygen and hydrogen. Its vibration and transformation depend on the surrounding temperature. Each form is independent of the others, and each has its unique qualities, benefits, purpose, and importance.

"This transformation is like that of one's soul. At the proper time, a spark of electrical energy in the heart of a developing physical body starts the heart to beat. At some point, the energy of the soul, which originates in the invisible Spirit Realm at a very high vibrational frequency, enters the visible Physical Realm in the heart of a developing human body at a low vibrational frequency.

"Later in life, when the electrical energy of the body ceases to function, physical death occurs. The soul energy releases from the body and shifts back to a very high frequency. Remember - it is a scientific fact that energy stays constant and only changes its form. The soul energy, invisible to those in the Physical Realm, returns to the high vibrational frequency of the Spirit Realm. This process is like changing a gas to a solid and, later, from a solid back to a gas. This process is also similar to changing frequencies of one radio station to another.

"The vibrational frequency is different on each level of the Spirit Realm. All souls living at the same vibrational frequency can see one another just as you can see each other in the Physical Realm. Each level, or frequency, is available to each soul and, once learned, the desired earned level is attainable whenever a soul changes frequency."

Rebecca looked over at me. "Does this make sense? Do you have questions?"

For a moment, I was speechless. "I am completely amazed at each comparison and explanation. I would never have thought of using water to explain this transformation. It was clear and, yes, I am surprised that I understand. I have no questions. In fact, it actually makes more sense than I expected, and it definitely answers several of my questions. Wow! Thank you."

"Okay, that's wonderful. It pleases me that you understand, but if you think of something, don't hesitate to ask. I will continue."

Rebecca: Water, Body, Mind, and Soul

"Here's another correlation between the body, mind, and soul and the transformation of water from solid to liquid to gas. You may need to use your imagination a little more for this one, though.

"The body is of the visible physical world, the material world. It is the outer, visible result of genetics and is how one presents oneself to the world. The visible body is firm and, therefore, has the lowest vibrational frequency. In this regard, the body correlates with the visible, solid state of water, which is ice.

"The soul within each person is of the unseen spirit world and corresponds to the invisible, gaseous plane of thought, the Divine, the highest vibrational frequency. This plane is above the fallacies and delusions of the physical world. The soul is inspirational and seeks perfection, clarity, and the ideal of all things. The soul seeks a broader view of life with peace, love, joy, strength, and wisdom. This invisible, spiritual state of the soul is elastic and can expand quickly and infinitely. Therefore, the soul correlates with the unseen, gaseous state of water vapor.

"The mind is the connecting link between the visible and the invisible, the intellectual and the inspirational, the solid and the gaseous. A thought is not entirely material or entirely spiritual. Thought vibrates between the two states - between the lowest vibrations of the solid physical body, the brain, and the highest vibrations of the gaseous-invisible spirit, the soul. Because of this connection, thoughts can be both intellectual and inspirational, and can easily flow between the solid and the gaseous states. In this way, the mind corresponds to the changing liquid state of water.

"Consciousness, awareness, control of the mind, and control of intentions are vitally important. The mind of every person is continually thinking. These thoughts and the resulting actions are often about physical well-being, about how to satisfy wants and needs, to survive, and to live a comfortable life in the material world.

"The thoughts that result in action are based on the five senses of the body and tend to originate from emotions. Impulsive thoughts seeking instant gratification may result from strong emotions, which would make it difficult to overcome impulsive temptations. When a person seeks a better life, feelings and actions bounce back and forth between the impulsive-physical and the inspirational-spiritual, between the visible solid state and the invisible gaseous state. Spontaneous ideas may become impulsive actions. Being aware of impulsive consequences and illogical decisions is very important in order to avoid future problems that may affect one's life.

"One can identify solutions once thoughts begin to flow easily between the lower and higher states. With determination and perseverance, it becomes easier to change the conditions of one's life using both the intellectual and inspirational liquid state of mind.

"Once significant changes are made and life becomes comfortable, it is easier to think about and look at a broader, grander view of life. Once one is not as preoccupied with obtaining the vital necessities for survival, thoughts and the imagination can soar above past concerns and dramas of the physical world. One no longer sees lack or limitation, only what is possible for the future.

"These thoughts originate from the soul combined with Divine intuition and inspiration. These grander thoughts are more about ideal conditions of life with limitless possibilities, along with inner peace, love, joy, strength, and wisdom. They are the highest thoughts of the soul, our Divine connection to God's essence within each of us. Because the soul correlates with the invisible, gaseous state of water, these thoughts can expand indefinitely.

"The mind chatter is constant. It is up to each person to listen to these thoughts, words, or stories being repeated over and over that help or hinder one's outlook and path in life. Are the thoughts optimistic or pessimistic? Are they reactive to circumstances without concern for possible consequences or responsive to what is best for all concerned? Are they about taking responsibility for any mistakes or wrong-doings that have occurred? Are thoughts about choices and changes to increase one's well-being; to alter attitudes and perspectives; or taking a different path in life? Ultimately, thoughts determine our beliefs, and our beliefs determine our actions. Our actions determine our outlook and path in life!

"Once a person notices the mental chatter and pays attention to the thoughts or stories being heard, it is up to each individual to control these thoughts. There is a mental energy flow between the lower vibrational, intellectual, impulsive thoughts of the material mind, and the higher vibrational, inspirational, responsive thoughts of the spiritual soul. Both are always present and important for any decision. At some point, though, on his or her path of life, the person may decide which one is more fulfilling and dominant, the material world of the mind or the spirit world of the soul.

"If a person decides that the physical, material world of outer results is more fulfilling, then hardship, confusion, chaos, doubt, fear, and guilt may or may not result. If a person decides that the spirit, invisible world of intuition is more fulfilling, then the person enters a higher state of mind above past concerns and dramas of the physical world. The person may then view life as filled with inspiration, clarity, and possibilities. There still may be hardships, confusion, chaos, doubt, fear, and guilt, but he or she may view the hardship as an opportunity to expand self-awareness and make changes instead of viewing hardships as obstacles or feeling like a victim to the circumstance."

"Also, during life, each person will have a deep need to find an unknown something that brings a feeling of satisfaction, fulfillment, and joy. One example is when people continually buy the biggest and best of everything, hoping this will bring happiness and fulfillment. The things may bring happiness for a short time, but the feeling of fulfillment is not long lasting, and the search continues, requiring the person to buy other things.

"Another example is when people continually keep themselves busy to avoid feeling or thinking about their deepest emotions. They may stay busy because they need to feel needed by other people. They may also do things or go places that result in instant gratification to feel happiness, joy, satisfaction, and fulfillment, but these are not long lasting either.

"Life in the Physical Realm continues with hardships and struggles. However, each person who recognizes the higher vibration of the soul can connect with it using intentional thought processes. Each person with faith and trust can ask for and receive Divine energy, focus, intuitions, and inspirations to supply the guidance, strength, and wisdom needed. The ability to perceive this energy increases with every choice to access the higher vibration, or higher consciousness. At some point, each person will have a profound realization that there are limitless possibilities in all things. This ability to access and receive Divine guidance and feel God's Unconditional Love is the long-term inner peace, satisfaction, fulfillment, and joy that everyone is searching for, whether realized or not.

Rebecca paused, and I remained silent, thinking about this information and the many different aspects and perspectives of life. She finally asked, "How are you doing? This correlation of the body, mind, and soul using the transformation of water as an example can be confusing to understand at first. Do these concepts make sense to you?"

"There's a lot to think about. You explained it well. I'm not sure if I'll remember all of this, though. There's so much, I don't even know what to ask!" I replied.

"When the time comes to remember and you are having difficulty, ask for guidance and it will be given. We are not allowed to interfere. You must remember to ask for help to remember, to understand, and for more clarity."

"Thank you, Rebecca! I'll definitely remember that! Yes, please continue by all means. This is fascinating!"

Rebecca: Water and the Law of Gravity

"Water follows the Law of Gravity. Water flows downward, showing that it is easier to shift to a lower energy level, or frequency, than to a higher level. This applies to each individual. Our consciousness is fluid, following the mind or heart. It is much easier to shift one's consciousness to a lower, more negative state of mind, or emotion, than to raise it to a more positive state of mind, or emotion. However, with focused intention, a shift to any level is possible using conscious awareness and intention.

"When you wish to expand conscious awareness, many things become possible. You can shift your energies, focus, and intention to connect to God or to whatever level or dimension within the Spirit Realm you desire. Praying is a wonderful example of this. After praying, pay attention to your heart, your breath, and your body. When the connection occurs, you will know it. You will feel a subtle shift of energy within and around your body. Take several deep breaths. You may feel a subtle relaxation and inner peace. You may even feel an unconscious sigh.

"There is a saying that water finds its own level. This also pertains to the vibrational frequency of each individual. Each person will resonate with a frequency that feels comfortable for one's self. One example of this is a group of like-minded friends or colleagues who all have similar beliefs and interests.

Once there is advancement of knowledge and understanding, there is an expansion of consciousness to a higher level of wisdom. Life may feel different. There may be a greater sense of responsibility and integrity. Vibrational frequency increases when focusing thoughts, words, and deeds on the new higher level of consciousness. Also, a desire for a new job or a promotion within the current job may occur.

"The opposite is also true. If there is no desire for advancement, if he or she resonates with the current vibrational frequency, and if one's life and consciousness level feel comfortable, life will remain the same. He or she will remain happy, comfortable, and content, feeling no need to change or expand.

"The physical body is 70% water, which helps to support balance within each of the body's organs and harmony among the complex functions of all the organs working together. Clearly, it is important to the vitality of the physical body to maintain a constant renewal of good-quality water. As previously said, the body can survive many days without food, but it cannot do so without water. Hopefully, the properties and the importance of water to all life will help people better understand that good-quality water is vital to life and not to take it for granted."

Rebecca smiled and asked, "This one's pretty easy. What do you think?"

I smiled back and nodded. "Yes, this one was the easiest to understand, with no need for questions. It's still interesting though. More of my questions are being answered which I am grateful for."

"Okay, this will be my last vital topic to cover. Here we go - Cause and Effect!"

Rebecca: Water, Cause and Effect, Action and Reaction

Rebecca took a deep, calming breath, smiled, and then continued. "This last correlation with water is significant because it illustrates cause and effect, or action and reaction. The waves of water are like waves of energy that radiate outward from each person to affect others or to bounce back to the point of origin.

"Any thought, word, or action has a wave of energy with a vibrational frequency that will cause an effect. It is an action with a corresponding reaction. It could be an act of kindness or an act of deceit, an act of love or one of hate or fear.

"Here's an example to visualize and even experiment with that may help you better understand this principle. If a pebble drops into the center of a bowl of water, you can see the vibrations of the water radiate out from the center in ever-widening circles. When the waves hit the rim of the bowl, they bounce back to the place where the pebble entered the water, the point of origin.

"In the Physical Realm, there is power behind every emotionally charged thought, word, and action from each individual everywhere. This power causes energetic vibrations to go outward from the point of origin in ever-widening circles into the energy of others, also called the collective consciousness. These intended vibrations will eventually cause an effect, or reaction, of the same high or low vibrational frequency. This effect, or reaction, may return quickly or may take years to return to the point of origin. The individual will then be subject to the reaction caused by those original thoughts, words, or actions, perceived as good or bad, love or fear.

"A person is responsible for what he or she thinks, says, and does. One example is the fact that a kind word or a loving action may eventually affect and help the sender. The actions of malicious gossiping, lying, or harmful behavior may eventually affect and harm the sender. The energy of the collective consciousness also eventually reflects the effect of energies, whether loving or harmful, of the majority of people within a group, community, state, country, and even the world."

"There is a conscious choice of how to control one's thoughts. Thoughts have power and energetic vibrations. Being mindful of the mental stories you tell yourself about yourself and others is more important than you can imagine. One's actions toward oneself and how one speaks to others, reflects one's beliefs and level of conscious awareness. One's actions can result in kindness, patience, understanding, compassion, forgiveness, respectfulness, and peaceful tolerance of all people. The opposite also applies. One's actions can also result in harmful behavior such as gossiping, cheating, lying, selfishness, greed, spitefulness, dishonesty, and being critical or judgmental.

"Every action has the potential to harm or to help. Each person's choices ultimately reveal the character or personality of that individual. Most of these choices lead to a philosophy of life and will determine whether the soul advances or not.

"There is purpose and meaning to everything we do, whether or not we realize it, even our good intentions that don't work out. With every lesson learned in life, one expands conscious awareness, gains knowledge, and has a better understanding of life. Better decisions and choices can result in wisdom and stronger boundaries, which can affect all aspects of one's life. Once you learn and truly understand these lessons, you will have an inner knowing that will forever remain within your soul, even when you have another lifetime in the Physical Realm."

Rebecca took another deep breath and smiled again. "Well, that completes my share of time and information with you. I know it's a lot to take in all at once. Are you completely confused or overwhelmed? Does this make sense to you? Do you understand?"

"Wow!" is all I could say for a few minutes. "All of this information makes sense to me and I'm understanding it as an overview, a higher perspective, of how everything and everyone are intertwined. It is a bit overwhelming. I never realized how the physical, mental, and emotional aspects of our lives completely affect others. Am I correct? What happens in life not only affects our individual souls but also the collective consciousness?"

"Yes, you are correct. It is the majority of people within the group, community, and so on that influence others in a positive or negative way that may eventually affect the consciousness of the whole. It is not so much every single thought, word, or deed in life, but each aspect of our life affects one's soul when the behavior repeats and becomes a pattern or a habit that can influence others around you. That's when one starts to realize and understand that there is a lesson to be learned.

"The pattern or a triggered event is the soul's way of helping one realize that something is off and needs to be investigated deep within the heart and soul. Once this personal investigation takes place and the lesson is discovered and learned, blockages can be released, self-knowledge is gained, and the soul realigns with God, Source Energy, and refills with higher energies. Consciousness increases and it becomes easier to make better choices."

Oh, my goodness, Rebecca. Thank you so much. Water was a wonderful medium to use for these examples. The correlations are easy to visualize and understand. What is next?"

"Matthew will be your next teacher/guide. He is from the Celestial Realm, one of the highest levels within the Spirit Realm. It's always an honor to be in the presence of anyone from the Celestial Realm. Remain here in this room and I will inform Matthew with telepathy that you are ready for him. Breathe deeply and relax. He will arrive soon. I bid you farewell."

"May Love, Peace, Faith, and Trust
flow like a river filling your soul always."

~ REBECCA ~

CHAPTER 5

Matthew: Spirit Realm

Rebecca departed and left me alone in the same dimly lit room. I sat quietly, breathing deeply, trying to relax, but still in awe of everything that had already happened.

Suddenly, the room became brighter. A mist gathered in the center of the room, and I stood up with much curiosity. There was a low swishing sound, and I felt a soft gentle breeze just before I saw a man appear where the mist had been. He was about six feet tall and wearing a floor-length white robe with a rope tied around his waist, similar to both Jacob and Robert. He looked similar to Robert, except his white hair and beard were much longer, both well below his shoulders. His cobalt-blue eyes were captivating. There was a soft glow of majestic light radiating around him. My first thought was that he definitely looked like a celestial being!

The man slowly walked over to me and introduced himself. "Greetings, Sharon. The name I go by is Matthew. I know Rebecca has already told you my name and that I live here in the Spirit Realm. It pleases us that you are here, and we hope to answer your questions about life in the Physical Realm so you can make a better informed decision about your future there.

"You have some remembrance of being in this energy of God's Unconditional Love between lifetimes, which is wonderful but is now causing you to question life in the Physical Realm. You are looking for the answers to the questions of 'Why is life this or that way?' These questions can occur each time you, or anyone, feel upsetting emotions, such as anxiety, confusion, grief, worry, or abandonment. Because you have some remembrance, you have an unconscious desire for everything to be perfect again, full of God's Divine Unconditional Love. It becomes upsetting to you when it is not so.

"We are all aware of how difficult it can be living in the third-dimensional physical world. There is no simple answer to a complex situation at this time. Each person returns for different reasons with different goals and intentions. Therefore, each person is at a different level of soul growth, soul evolution, and spiritual maturity. These are a few answers, but the 'why' questions are the reason you are here. You are quite inquisitive and very persistent! However, we did not want you to make the mistake of taking your life again, since this is an important life for you.

"Hopefully, after learning how the vibrational frequencies of energy work within both the Physical and Spirit Realms and then how they relate to each other, you will have a better understanding of the 'why' questions. Hopefully, this information will also help you learn about and better understand the purpose and meaning of life in the Physical Realm while you are still living there and enjoying your life.

"Does that make sense to you? Or should I say, do you understand what I mean?"

Feeling love radiating from him, I smiled and replied. "Thank you, Matthew. Knowing that I have some remembrance of the energy of God's Unconditional Love probably answers my most important question of all! No wonder I had a difficult time accepting a life of struggle and hardship in the Physical Realm. Not understanding how and why people could do such terrible things to each other was worst of all.

"Knowledge obtained from Jacob, Robert, and Rebecca has answered many other questions and has helped a great deal so far. Understanding how things work on an energy level in both the Physical and Spirit Realms is amazing. I am so grateful for this information. Please continue."

Matthew smiled back and began speaking. "You are welcome, and I am pleased that you are starting to have a better understanding through expanded awareness." Matthew paused a moment. "I do hope, though, that you realize all the previous information has been greatly simplified. You are nodding your head. I hope that means you understand that there is much more to all of this. We don't want to overwhelm you, so try to think of this as an overview of the intricacies of both realms."

"Yes, I do realize that. I'm sure it's just the basics, but I am still in awe of it all and appreciate this opportunity!"

Wonderful! You are welcome. It is our pleasure to be of service at all times. I shall continue with a little more about the Spiritual Realm."

"One of the highest frequencies in the Spirit Realm is the Celestial level close to the consciousness of God, Great Spirit, the Divine, Source Energy, Life Force, or "ALL That Is." There are many more names, but all of them refer to the highest frequency of all. It is impossible for people on Earth to understand the complete beauty, balance, purity, and perfection of the highest levels of the Spirit Realm.

"Those living in the Celestial frequency receive the highest teachings, revealing most mysteries. Many teachers/guides from that level come here to this first level of the Spirit Realm to teach and guide anyone ready to receive instruction - usually intuitively, but sometimes by personal contact, as it is now for you. When this occurs, it is possible to see and hear the teachers/guides perfectly, although your frequency is much lower. It is by the very presence and radiant energy of a Celestial being that the consciousness and vibrational frequency of the space and those in it rise high enough for you to see, hear, and speak to them perfectly, just as you see, hear, and speak with people on Earth.

"As Robert said earlier, there are many levels of existence and many dimensions in the Spirit Realm. Each successively higher level is brighter, more beautiful, and more wondrous than the level below, due to increased knowledge and understanding. The higher the conscious awareness of someone living on Earth, the more one will feel and see the beauty, balance, harmony, order, and connection of all living things in the physical world.

"At this time, it is impossible for those in the Physical Realm to fully comprehend the complexities, the perfection, and the complete Unconditional Love that exists for all life on all levels and dimensions within this vast Universe. The good news is that we are all spiritually connected to this Divine force, whether or not people realize and believe it.

"The high-frequency energy of the atmosphere in the Spirit Realm is the energy of Unconditional Love. The air is inspirational and full of energy. There are feelings of peace, love, joy, freedom, and even bliss. Instead of breathing oxygen, you breathe the ever-present, unlimited Divine Unconditional Love. You were correct when you were first here. It pleased us that you felt it and realized what you were feeling.

"Also, within the Spirit Realm, there is an awareness of all thoughts, motives, desires, and actions of everyone by everyone. There are no secrets. There is no need to hide anything, deceive, take advantage, or have power over anyone. All give respect to all. This truth is the same on each level of the Spirit Realm. By knowing the thoughts and feelings of newly arrived souls, a teacher/guide can evaluate the level of knowledge, understanding, and wisdom of each returning soul. They provide the best response to each question at the proper level of understanding. Specific examples and illustrations can help the person understand the answer better, creating an open, clear channel of information.

"Pure spiritual growth, or soul growth, occurs on all levels. What one learns here in the Spirit Realm is put into practice in the physical world, but unfortunately, without conscious awareness of the knowledge gained here. However, the soul stores the knowledge within. That is the meaning of "everything you need is within." In moments of deep contemplation, meditation, shamanic journeys, or dreams, one may glimpse this deeper wisdom. When asking God for guidance in moments of openness, sit quietly in the stillness and listen. Be open to hear or sense a response and allow it to enter your heart. It may not be what you want, but it will be what your soul needs.

"As spiritual growth increases through knowledge, understanding, and wisdom, there is an evolution of the soul. The higher the level or frequency you reach, the higher the level at which you will live while in the Spirit Realm.

"Also, in the Spirit Realm, there is music around us at all times, even though others cannot hear it. It is low in volume, so you must become quiet and raise your level of conscious awareness. While in the quietness, listen intently with intention and you will hear this incredible, beautiful, uplifting music. It is the sound of harmony within the Spirit Realm and is always present. This majestic music is relaxing, comforting, and inspirational. I know you have heard it. Enjoy listening whenever you can."

Matthew: Spirit Realm, Soul Energy

"When one passes through the doorway of transition, there is an automatic transformation of soul energy, frequency, time, and space. The energy of the soul usually transitions to this first level of the Spirit Realm, as Robert spoke about earlier. The power of the mind, scientific laws and principles, and the Universal Forces of God controls the energy of the soul which functions in both realms. One can achieve a higher level of consciousness by aligning one's mind and soul to higher thoughts, feelings, and perspectives.

"As a soul in spirit masters the ability to transform one's soul energy with intention, there can be a change in vibrational frequency and conscious awareness. This allows each soul to shift its energies to other levels within the spirit world. However, the soul energy is only allowed to shift to a previously earned level of higher consciousness while still in spirit. If one chooses to lower his or her frequency, one can also connect with the physical world. Depending on the level of one's energy and power, the surrounding energy field may or may not be affected. Sensitive people in the physical world may feel the energy, while others may also see the image of the spirit.

"The power and intention of the mind become the doorway to higher consciousness, higher vibrational frequencies, and higher levels of knowledge, understanding, and wisdom. This is also true while still living in the Physical Realm. When properly used and aligned with the Universal Forces of God, the possibilities are limitless. One may transport from one location to another by willing it to happen. Also, one may communicate with another person at any distance by telepathy.

"The powers of this energy allow one in the physical world to master the abilities of telepathy, intuition, channeling, healing, psychic abilities, and more. Once mastered, these abilities stay within the soul to be used in future lifetimes in the Physical Realm. We usually consider them gifts of the soul, which help to explain child prodigies."

Matthew: Spirit Realm, Shift from Spirit to Physical Realm

Matthew glanced at me to see if I wanted to say something. I was shaking my head, implying no. He smiled and continued speaking.

"As just discussed, souls in the Spirit Realm on all levels can shift or transform to other frequency levels, including the Physical Realm. This shift happens for many reasons, especially when souls can be of service to those in the physical world who are trying to understand life or who need spiritual comfort. Prayer may also summon emotional support from those in Spirit in times of need.

"The specific purpose of many spirit guides is to support people in the Physical Realm, but also souls of deceased friends, relatives, or angels may help too. Spirits can see and hear people in the physical world, can see life from a much broader perspective, and are aware of the many activities and struggles that occur during physical life. Souls in spirit may want to see the lives of loved ones, especially during significant times in life. They may want to comfort loved ones and, occasionally, may make their presence known. They may then bring comfort, a message, or other information to a friend or loved one in some unique manner that is known only to that friend or loved one in order to identify themselves.

"For those in the physical world in need of support, there may be a thought, or concept, or visual experience downloaded into the mind of the person asking. One of the most common ways souls in spirit make contact is by manipulating electricity, such as making the telephone ring, but no one is calling. Another is when spirits enter the dream state to speak to their loved ones in the physical world to offer support. The dreamer may perceive this spirit-inspired dream as a 'great dream' with unusual real-life qualities.

"When someone is dying and about to transition back to Spirit, an angel, guide, or a soul in the Spirit Realm may visit the Physical Realm. Sometimes, the soul energy of departed family members, close friends, or others will comfort the dying person and help him or her transition with ease and grace. People still living and present at the time of their loved one's death may or may not perceive the energy of these souls in spirit being there to help."

"Once the transition occurs, it is possible that the soul now in Spirit may contact someone in the Physical Realm a short time after his or her physical death. This contact may continue periodically for an indeterminate amount of time. The need for this contact may decrease or cease as souls in both realms grow and continue on their path along their life's journey.

"Any of these actions of support may answer questions, help a friend or loved one identify a solution to a problem, or help him or her visualize a future that could result from different choices.

"Other examples of support from the Spirit Realm are when one often finds specific coins, sees a certain type of bird or butterfly, or hears a lyric from a favorite song, which triggers a memory. Each of these can bring a sense of inner peace to a grieving person or to someone who needs spiritual help. However, many people in the Physical Realm do not realize this possibility."

Matthew: Spirit Realm, Physical Lifetimes

"During life in the Physical Realm, the spirit, or soul memory, is suppressed but not erased. Each person may realize, or simply know, certain spiritual truths but not fully understand how or why he or she feels that way. This realization can result from memories stored within the subconscious and super-conscious mind. Also, unexplained thoughts, feelings, visions, or dream experiences can be Divine inspirations from God, or from teachers, guides, or other souls within the Spirit Realm.

"Each person is always connected to God through his or her soul, whether or not realized. If one makes a conscious connection of mind to heart to soul, one's physical life will usually be joyful, peaceful, and content as one pursues his or her dreams and desires. Without a conscious connection, one usually ignores dreams and desires of the heart, which may result in a less joyful life of unfulfillment, unhappiness, and discontent. One learns life lessons from either way of life, especially when practicing self-analysis. One gains wisdom with each better choice.

"Think of the body as the vehicle for one's lifetime and the soul as the driver of one's inner mental, emotional, and spiritual life. Prior to the soul returning to the Physical Realm, arrangements are made to supply the greatest number of opportunities of experience to advance the conscious awareness of the person. Once the heart and soul connect, the soul will attract certain situations to the individual, which are necessary for the predetermined lessons to be learned. The soul will also attract to the individual conditions that will fill one's life with Love, Light, and Blessings to help overcome obstacles as one pursues dreams and desires.

"When one begins to think of obstacles as opportunities to learn life lessons, one gains knowledge, understanding, and wisdom about one's self. The level of awareness, consciousness, and soul energy will expand significantly. Recognizing a recurring problem and a pattern of behavior will become apparent. After objective self-analysis from a higher perspective, awareness of long-term behavior becomes clear, making it easier to understand how and why the pattern occurred. Changing personal thoughts, beliefs, and perspectives is then necessary to change the old unconscious habitual behavior.

"Each lesson learned becomes the means to reach a personal goal, whether it be mental, emotional, physical, or spiritual. The knowledge and understanding gained is a small step toward obtaining the final goal. Clarity and wisdom increase each time, adding to one's strength, power, and confidence to make different choices to change future actions in order to bring about a different desired condition.

"The direction of one's thoughts becomes the direction of one's actions. A person truly learns a lesson only by changing his or her behavior and thoughts.

If not, conditions will remain the same as before. Similar patterns of life will repeat until one learns the lesson and actions change.

"It is important not to get stuck in the hardship and struggle of the lesson itself. Instead, hold on to the vision of the goal, knowing that the only purpose of the lesson is to increase knowledge and understanding of one's self to achieve the highest goal."

"The Physical Realm has a great deal of drama and chaos if there is no balance and harmony. As one learns life lessons, there is greater understanding. The wisdom gained from these lessons does not have to be through tragedy and heartache. One gains knowledge and learns lessons by listening to others' experiences, seeing all aspects of life, and recognizing the wisdom within each situation. The understanding and wisdom of the lesson are then put into practice. Each realization and accomplishment advances soul growth and increases personal power, or soul energy.

"As one evolves from the material to more of the spiritual, values and priorities change. Being helpful to others becomes more important than being served by others. Material possessions become less important. There is more balance in life. Also, one continues to learn and grow in the ways of Spirit, to become more productive, capable, and responsible for one's self and for the influence we may have on other individuals. When there is sufficient soul growth, there is also advancement to higher levels once in the Spiritual Realm."

After another pause and a deep relaxing breath, Matthew said, "Well, that completes my contribution to explaining some of the things that go on here in the Spirit Realm. Do you understand? Do you need more explanations?"

"No." I replied. "Actually, my mind is spinning. You explained it well and am pretty sure I understand the basics. There's a lot more to this than I could ever imagine. It's all so amazing!"

Matthew laughed a little and said, "That is not surprising. It is not the first time I have heard that comment, either. You have two more teachers/guides that will enlighten you about nature and human nature, Benjamin and Francis. Then you will see Jacob again for the final wrap-up.

"It is a pleasure to meet you, Sharon. We hope we answered your questions, and that you gained a broader perspective of life, death, love, peace, and joy on Earth and in the heavens. Hopefully, you will make a more informed decision and reconsider the outcome of your current life in the physical world.

"I will leave you now. Benjamin is waiting for you. Stay here and relax. Close your eyes and take a few deep relaxing breaths. Visualize a beam of White Light going from you to Benjamin on the edge of a nearby forest. Imagine a beautiful warm sunny day. See yourself there outside next to the forest. Relax and take three deep breaths. Then breathe normally and relax."

"May the Light of God surround you.
May the Love of God fill your heart.
May the Will of God bring you clarity.
May the Blessings of God flow to you with ease and grace."

~ MATTHEW ~

CHAPTER 6

Benjamin: Nature, Trees, Energy, Parallels

Matthew turned to walk away but disappeared after just a few steps. His disappearance startled me, but after remembering how he arrived, I smiled to myself and was no longer surprised. I followed Matthew's instructions and told myself to relax, close my eyes, and take several deep breaths. Then breathe normally while I imagine the beam of White Light. See myself travel there outside next to the forest with Benjamin. Relax.

Suddenly, I felt a warm gentle breeze on my cheek like a soft kiss. My eyes opened to see a meadow filled with vibrantly colored wildflowers on the edge of a forest. Wow, was all I could think to say to myself over and over once again. I loved this amazing new way of traveling. Just inside the woods, I saw a man walking toward me carrying a tall walking stick. He looked about six feet tall, in his thirties, and physically fit. This man had dark skin and shoulder-length dark brown hair with a short mustache and beard wearing a tunic type shirt, loose-fitting pants, and boots laced up over the bottom of his pants.

As he came closer, I saw a big smile on his face. He said, "Hi there. My name is Benjamin. It is nice to meet you."

Smiling, I walked toward him and replied, "Thank you, Benjamin. It's definitely a pleasure to meet you. I can't tell you how much I appreciate receiving all this remarkable information. Being here in the Spirit Realm is something I could never have imagined. Matthew told me there would be two more teachers/

guides that would talk about nature and human nature. I'm assuming you are the first one."

"Yes, you are correct. I am the first teacher/guide today to talk about my favorite topic, Nature. My goal is to help increase your awareness and understanding of the energies of nature by comparing plant life with human life. Shall we go sit under that large oak tree over there on the edge of the forest to continue our talk?"

I nodded and followed. We sat in the tree's shade and Benjamin continued. "As you can see, the great outdoors is the best example of the majestic beauty of Nature. Plant life and human life both supply many examples of cycles of transformation. By comparing these cycles from a higher, more objective perspective, one gains a deeper knowledge and understanding of the cycles of life, including the cycle of life and death. There are also cycles within cycles. These observations may expand one's awareness of God's presence, decrease fear of death, and help one find purpose and meaning in life.

"Nature is the entire physical universe. All things in it are of God and from God. Its beauty is God's way of displaying love for us. Nature can be the teacher of life lessons for all people on many levels at all times. It renews one's connection to faith, hope, trust, and love of life itself. There are lessons to learn and wisdom to be found everywhere one looks, from the clouds above to the grain of sand below. Nature illustrates God's Universal Laws of balance, moderation, harmony, and order in all kingdoms - human, plant, animal, and mineral. It's always best to experience Nature in its purest form, if possible. To see the displays of magnificent beauty everywhere one looks, to feel the healing energies that radiate to all from Mother Nature, and to receive the many blessings bestowed to all - can be life-changing.

"There is a quote that we believe is true and used often by Ralph Waldo Emerson: *In the woods, we return to reason and faith.*" Another quote we love is, *Come forth into the light of things. Let Nature be your teacher,*" by William Wordsworth.

"There are different plants, flowers, trees, vines, and shrubs that I can use as examples. Trees are the easiest to compare with human life since almost everyone is familiar with them. Trees are gentle giants and magnificent specimens to behold. They are our silent companions packed with patience and wisdom, just waiting for us to ask the right question in order to tap into that wisdom. Believe it or not, there are many concepts and lessons to be learned from them that can help us understand our human lives better.

"Each tree has its unique characteristics, such as leaves, bark, fruit, roots, benefits, and purpose. The benefits depend on the type of tree, such as fruit or nuts. Some people use the leaves, bark, or roots for medicinal purposes. Each of these examples helps to fulfill the purpose of the tree supplying a benefit to others, both human and animal."

"The life of a tree parallels the life of a person. Trees begin life from a seed. Within each seed, there is a blueprint for the tree's growth, development, and all its characteristics, such as leaves, flowers, buds, and bark.

"Similarly, human life begins with a seed having DNA and RNA. This seed includes directions for each individual's growth and the development of his or her characteristics, such as height, bone structure, and the color of hair, skin, and eyes.

"The life of each person also has unique abilities, skills, and characteristics. People everywhere have similarities and everyday basic needs. Each individual uses these unique abilities as best he or she can to give one's life passion, purpose, and meaning. Each person may also supply a service for others, either through employment, volunteering, friendship, or service to others. This service helps the person and his or her family, friends, community, and possibly the world."

"There are many lessons to learn when there is an awareness of the purpose of each part of a tree within the more extensive system. Let's use the deciduous oak tree we are sitting under as an example. When you look at the tree, you see the exterior of a physical object. The tree is growing or dormant, but it's impossible to see the functions of any other part within the tree. It could be absorbing water in the roots, performing photosynthesis in the leaves, or transporting and distributing nutrients under its outer woody sheath. We see only the outside of the tree.

"The same concept applies to a person, although each individual is much more complicated than a tree. When one looks at a person, the body is all that is seen. It is impossible to know what is taking place within a person's physical body from outward appearances. It is the same for each person's mental, emotional, and spiritual state of well-being, along with his or her personal and professional life. There may be physical pain, mental anguish, emotional heartache, and personal or professional challenges known only to the individual.

"We can learn several lessons from this observation. Some people are quick to criticize, make fun of, or judge others. The most significant lesson is a greater awareness of challenges within a person's life that are not known to others. One may then consciously become more patient, considerate, respectful, and compassionate to every person one meets."

Benjamin stopped speaking and looked at me. "Are these comparisons difficult to understand or relate to? Is this anything you observed before? Any questions?

"No, I've never considered these comparisons before. I love nature and trees, so it all makes sense to me. The information feels relatable, and I think it's great to observe the intricacies of life from a much different perspective. Yes, I see many people who are critical and judgemental about others they know nothing about. This is a different and interesting way to see others."

Benjamin looked happy and said, "Thank you. Yes, when you see the big picture and feel neutral about life and nature, it's easy to see how things relate to each other. I am pleased that you agree."

Benjamin: Trees ~ Purpose and Connection

"Since you have no questions, I'll continue. The life of deciduous trees is the easiest for most people to understand. It is a perfect example to compare the life of a tree with human life. By only using the example of this large oak tree we are sitting under, I hope you understand this information applies to all trees.

"The balance, moderation, harmony, and order found in Nature show how every part of the whole has its place, fulfills a specific purpose, and functions independently within the whole. Each part connects with a larger part of the whole, becoming progressively more complex. Each part by itself may seem small or insignificant. However, it is not. Each part must function properly to support the equilibrium and life of the whole.

"Here is an example of that. Think of one cell from one leaf on a deciduous oak tree. It takes many cells to make up each leaf. There are also veins within the leaf that bring water and nutrients to each cell. Chemical reactions occur with different sugars and chlorophyll to produce food or energy for the cell. There are also reactions to convert carbon dioxide into oxygen.

"It takes many leaves to make up a branch on the tree, many branches to make up a limb, and many limbs to complete the entire tree. The tree depends on each part to function properly for the life of the tree to continue. When all the leaves of a tree are combined, the amount of energy produced sustains the life of the tree. Each tree has the potential to supply many benefits.

"Now, think of a small forest. Think about its benefits to the surrounding area, including the animals and the landowner. Next, think about a vast forest and its benefits to the community, state, country, and possibly the world. This ultimately depends on having each cell of each part of the tree function properly.

"Here is an example that illustrates the workings of the human body in similar ways. Let's use one tissue cell from the heart. Each cell has a specific purpose and connects to all other cells found within the heart. The proper functioning of each cell is essential. It is one of many organs within the body, each with a specific purpose. The heart is independent of the other organs, but its proper functioning is vital to all organs.

"When the heart functions correctly, the life of the body continues. Each life has the potential to supply many benefits for itself and others. Think of all the possible contributions a person may offer to family, friends, neighbors, colleagues, and ultimately, to a culture, community, state, country, and even the world. Ultimately, each physical body depends on each cell to function properly.

"Within the whole of humanity, each person, like the single-cell, is independent and has a specific purpose. Although connected to all others, he or she has free will and makes many choices during his or her lifetime. Each person contributes to humanity whether realized or not. Some people seem to be more important than others and stand out from the rest. However, each person is just as important as the others. Each person plays a vital role functioning on his or her level of conscious awareness gained from learning life lessons. Each person strives to be the best person they can be. The lesson to be learned is that each person is ultimately important to all of humanity."

Benjamin took a deep breath, stopped speaking, and looked at me. "Were you able to follow that? Do you understand? Any questions or comments?"

"Yes, I was able to follow you, but it took a few minutes to understand. Once I visualized what you were saying, I saw it from a different perspective, as you would say - more in principle than literally. I have no questions yet."

"Very good. That's exactly the intention of comparing the life of a tree with human life. It is wonderful to see similarities in a deeper, more abstract way rather than literally. Now, we will explore another way to see Nature."

Benjamin: Trees ~ Cycles, and Cycles within Cycles

"Within Nature, there are many cycles, large and small. The most obvious cycle is the solar system and the orbit of the Earth around the Sun. It takes one full year to complete this cycle, resulting in four seasons: summer, fall, winter, and spring. Then there is the rotation of the Earth itself. This cycle takes one day, or 24 hours, to complete, resulting in our day and night. Because of the cycle of our four seasons and the daily cycle of the Earth, there is constant movement and constant change.

"The daily cycle of the Earth is an example of a cycle within a larger cycle of the four seasons. Another cycle within a cycle is the growth cycle that occurs during the life of all deciduous trees, such as this mighty oak tree. Each year, there is a new growth of leaves, supplying fresh energy to nourish the tree so that it becomes stronger, taller, and broader. The new growth matures and bears fruit. The fruit then matures and dies, producing seeds that will propagate new tree growth. Each year, the cycle of new growth helps the tree until it ends with the death of the leaves. These dead leaves then fall to the ground and replenish the soil with organic substances that will eventually nourish the tree. This cycle continues each year until the tree dies.

"One observation of the tree during the yearly cycle is that the tree does not die each year, only the new growth dies. While the tree is dormant during the winter months, the trunk and all of its branches appear to be dead, but they are not. As long as the tree lives, there is new growth each spring, just as fresh as its first year of growth. The tree becomes larger, stronger, and more magnificent with each growth cycle. Counting and measuring the tree trunk's growth rings reveals the number and quality of these cycles. One ring represents a one-year growth cycle. The width of each growth ring is proportional to the water, nutrition, and growing conditions of that particular year.

"One growth cycle of the tree is comparable to one person's lifetime. Each lifetime is a single growth cycle of the soul, or Spirit. When a person dies, the soul does not die. The soul within the body also appears to be dead, but it is not. The energy of the soul merely shifts - changing its frequency, or form, back to Spirit. Lessons learned during each lifetime nourish the soul, or Spirit, and add to its growth. Each new lifetime is just as new and just as separate as all earlier lifetimes. Also, during each lifetime, there is a possibility to bear children who will mature and pass along inherited DNA and RNA to continue the cycle."

"The life-cycle of a person is much more complicated than that of a plant or tissue cell. To find one's particular purpose within the whole, one must first gain knowledge. As each person matures, he or she learns more about life, strengths, and weaknesses. Recognizing priorities in one's life helps to set standards and boundaries. Also, realizing what brings happiness, awakens dreams and desires, and then taking steps to achieve those dreams. Each person chooses a path that gives passion, purpose, and meaning to life. A particular purpose usually involves something that one loves to do or wants to achieve in life. In time, one may become more responsible to one's self and to others. Each person may eventually realize one's significance to family, friends, and co-workers. Also, one may learn how personal choices can influence many people in multiple ways.

"The life-cycle of the soul reflects the number of mental, emotional, and spiritual lessons learned, how influential and important one is to others, and possibly to the world. If the actions in an earlier lifetime were primarily negative, each lifetime after that may suffer the consequences. These consequences will occur until one learns lessons through positive actions and behavior changes. This may take many lifetimes. If there is no change in behavior, soul growth remains the same.

"Each lifetime affects the next lifetime. Talents and abilities reappear as likes, dislikes, skills, talents, hobbies, or careers. Each consecutive lifetime is an opportunity to advance abilities in one or more fields of choice. An example is when a young person shows a unique ability to play an instrument with little or no training in the current lifetime. Each successive lifetime will reap the rewards and benefits of earlier lifetimes and will remain part of the soul as a cycle of positive growth."

"Knowledge gained, talents refined, and skills learned all stay part of the soul and may advance with each successive lifetime. This progression will continue until the soul is perfected and stays in Spirit. The soul never dies.

"Once there is soul growth and prosperity beyond life's needs to survive in the physical world, there may be financial success and advancement in most areas of life. Extra time and money may present other opportunities in life. There may be more concern for the welfare of others and a willingness and desire to help in some way.

"Another even higher purpose may present itself that may help many people, or humanity. However, to reach this point, many lessons are learned through experience, knowledge, and hardship. Each person is then more apt to have greater awareness, compassion, joy, and contentment with life. He or she ultimately realizes, and is grateful for, the many gifts and blessings received during his or her lifetime. The most significant benefit of all is consciousness, soul growth, and advancement to a higher level of understanding and wisdom.

"Growth cycles and life-cycles present us with an expanded awareness of thoughts we think, beliefs we have about ourselves, and actions we take. Ultimately, our conscious decision about each choice we make determines whether or not there is soul growth in each lifetime. The comparison of growth rings of a tree to life-cycles of the soul can help us understand that each lifetime is significant. Some people think that this may be the ultimate incentive program for soul evolution in order to have future lifetimes full of love, peace, joy, and happiness."

"One learns many life-lessons if one spends time in Nature. Nature may broaden conscious awareness and expand one's ability to feel energy, peace, and soul renewal. Observe the balance and harmony within every aspect of Nature, large and small. See how each aspect relates to the overall design, plan, or system you are observing. Only then will one be able to recognize the lesson and the wisdom found in it. Only then will one be able to compare and apply that same energy of balance, harmony, knowledge, understanding, and wisdom to your own life."

Benjamin paused, looked at me, and took a deep breath. He laughed a little and said, "I love this subject and tend to go on and on. I hope you understood my comparisons. The knowledge of how things work in Nature makes a big difference when we objectively observe the big picture. Being able to see how some systems relate to human life is challenging but also rewarding. Any comments?"

I laughed a little and quickly replied, "This is very interesting. I'm amazed at how much of this information makes sense to me. It's also surprising how important it is to learn life lessons. Reincarnation was never a belief of mine, but I was familiar with it. Actually, reincarnation now answers many of my questions. I'm astonished how much there is to observe in Nature, especially what's right in front of us we rarely pay attention to, like the cycles within cycles.

Are there more comparisons? This new awareness definitely helps me see things differently and with deeper meanings."

"I am pleased you are open to hearing alternate ways to interpret what you see. Yes, there are two more comparisons to be made, also with trees."

Benjamin: Trees and Tree Roots

"The next comparison involves tree roots. The roots of each tree are underground, unable to be seen. Everyone knows the roots are there nourishing the tree with water and nutrients, but are invisible to the eye. The deeper the roots, the larger, older, and more stable is the tree. The tree becomes stronger each year, enabling it to sway through high winds without uprooting.

"This situation is similar to that of our body and soul. Like the tree, the body is visible. The soul is spirit and is invisible. The soul compares to the roots, the foundation and stability of the tree. The roots of the soul are composed of faith, hope, love, and trust that each person has for God, or the Divine. The roots of the tree compare to our soul's connection to the Divine within. The deeper the roots of the soul, the easier it is to adapt to changes and challenges in life.

"After having spiritual experiences and learning many life lessons, one's spiritual awareness increases. The roots of the soul, one's foundation, grow larger and deeper, helping one become stronger and wiser. One is better equipped to weather the storms of one's life with ease and grace."

Benjamin paused a minute or two, thinking about something, and then continued. "The mind, the brain, is physical, material. The soul is invisible, spiritual. Remember, the mind is intellectual, and the soul is inspirational. When shifting consciousness from the mind to the heart and soul, there is a connection between both worlds. It is then possible for decisions and choices in all aspects of life to be balanced between the intellectual and inspirational perspectives. Responses to life's challenges will reflect the connection to the soul, the foundation, and the mind, adding strength, courage, knowledge, and understanding when making difficult decisions.

"Each person moves freely during life, vibrating at his or her unique frequency. Each has a different amount of accumulated soul energy. This energy increases by learning life lessons from observation or from struggles and hard-ships. With each lesson learned, conscious awareness and understanding of one's personal patterns also increase. At some point, one realizes that balanced decisions of the material and the spiritual become more dependable with faith, hope, love, and trust. One can apply the wisdom gained and reap the benefits of well-being, happiness, contentment, and accomplishment. The struggles may then seem to lessen or disappear one by one."

Benjamin: Single Tree vs. Cluster vs. Forest

"Okay, I promise that this is the last comparison between trees and humanity! Have you ever noticed how a single tree growing by itself is larger, fuller, and more uniform, with balanced growth on all sides? How does the growth of a cluster of trees appear? How do trees within a forest compare to the single tree or cluster of trees?

"Let's use the growth of an apple tree to compare a single tree to one person. The basic needs of the apple tree for survival are water, sunlight, nutrient-rich soil, and room to grow. A single tree has the benefit of receiving all the water, sunlight, and nutrients found within its root space. As a result, it grows to its greatest ability in height and width. It is perfectly balanced, receiving everything needed at all times from all directions. It not only survives, but also produces the largest amount of fruit possible for that particular tree. As a result, this apple tree illustrates what is possible when given the best conditions while helping both animals and humans.

"A cluster of apple trees is like a family unit. The dynamics are different for each. There will be competition, or a power struggle, among the trees for water, sunlight, nutrients, and space needed to fulfill the purpose of producing apples. Each separate tree must compromise and share the area, receiving only a part of what is available. Although each tree survives, produces fruit, and stays separate from the other trees, it never reaches its greatest growth or fruit capacity. At the same time, each tree helps to support the other trees within the cluster, functioning as an essential part of the cluster.

"A forest of trees compares to a city of people. The dynamics change again. The competition among the trees for water, sunlight, nutrients, and space is greater than in a cluster of trees. There are more trees in the same space, resulting in greater competition and more power struggles. However, each tree supports the other trees and still is an essential part of the entire forest.

"A single apple tree compares to one person. Each individual is unique, vibrates at a unique frequency, has a different soul energy level. Each person receives and absorbs the largest amount of energy available at all times. As a result, when spiritually mature, each person becomes a balanced specimen, demonstrating what is possible when given the greatest conditions. One can then help all those they come into contact with.

"Each person can experience and learn lessons alone, within a small group, in a large organization, or in a combination of these. There are many benefits for each. A person who is alone due to circumstances, or who chooses to be alone, learns lessons independently. When learning alone, there is less support from others, but there may be less competition to influence or distract from learning life lessons. A person learns lessons through struggles and hardships, or through observation and applied wisdom. Faith, hope, love, and trust in God, the Divine, or Source Energy, may also continue to increase in any situation.

"Both the family unit and the city of people can be either supportive or destructive to one another at different times in one's life. There may be competition and power struggles within the dynamics of each relationship, which may be disturbing and distracting. As a result of these complicated relationships, each one learns many life lessons. A few examples are respect, trust, loyalty, sharing duties, listening, and gaining new perspectives through compromise. When there are distractions and influences from many people, there may be confusion and a weaker connection with Spirit, leading to feelings of less power, less self-worth, and less self-confidence.

"One of the most challenging lessons is learning to stop the compulsion to control others or situations. One must remember that by choosing not to control others or a situation, one still is in control of him or herself. He or she also controls whether to have a knee-jerk reaction or to have a balanced response to others in any situation.

"Another example of a tough lesson to learn is the ability to put the welfare of others before that of oneself. To willingly serve others without expectation of reward is true charity. When one realizes that the more significant benefit of this action is to oneself rather than to others, there is soul growth.

The source of one's energy is God. This energy is always available to everyone equally when there is a clear connection to the Divine. Each person may make this connection by meditating, being in Nature, saying prayers, appreciating art, listening to music, exercising, or anything that brings one to a quiet, relaxing, inner space. This spiritual connection can renew and revive one's soul energy, reigniting one's passion and purpose, which gives meaning to one's life, whether alone or in a multitude."

There was silence for a moment. Before he could speak again, I said, "The parallels between trees and humans are fascinating. I'll have to think about several of them a little more, but I think I understand most of them. Being able to visualize and compare each of the examples is a great way to observe from an objective viewpoint. I'm speechless. Thank you, Benjamin, for opening my mind and soul to this information."

With a smile and gentle laugh, Benjamin graciously replied, "Thank you for being open enough to listen and allow a new understanding. Because you have new beliefs, you may view life differently from now on if you choose to remain in the physical world. We are hoping this information helps to answer more of your questions, that you reconsider your decision, and choose to remain on Earth. It was a pleasure meeting you."

"May the Spirit of Nature fill you with its Beauty,
Blessings, Mystery, and Infinite Love Always."

~ BENJAMIN ~

CHAPTER 7

Francis: Nature and the Animals

As Benjamin finished, I noticed another man a short distance away walking slowly through the woods. He held a tall walking stick and had a large cloth bag hanging over his shoulder. Benjamin and I stood up and noticed him scattering black sunflower seeds from his bag for the birds, squirrels, and chipmunks. He looked similar to Benjamin in age and appearance. His smiling face radiated happiness and love of the outdoors, especially for the animals.

When he reached us, we happily greeted him. Benjamin put his hand on this man's shoulder and said, "Let me introduce you to my good friend Francis, who is your next teacher/guide."

Benjamin and I sat back down under the shade of the oak tree while Francis remained standing. Francis paused a moment before speaking with great excitement. "Greetings! It is always nice to see Benjamin, and it is very nice to meet you, Sharon. It is my pleasure being here today. As discussed earlier, Nature is of God and all animals are part of Nature. The Laws of the Universe, or Cosmic Laws, demonstrate the Laws of Nature. These laws apply to all systems and help define the interaction of energy in all forms of life. Every aspect of Nature can teach something.

"Benjamin's specialty is plant life with an emphasis on trees. My specialty is also Nature, but is about animals, wild, domesticated, and even insects. Learning lessons from Nature must include animals. By seeing each animal's diverse characteristics, you can make limitless correlations between animals and human nature.

"My goal today is to compare animal and human behaviors. By applying some of the survival behaviors of animals to humans, it may be possible to create more order, balance, and harmony in the lives of people. Being open to and allowing conditions to change may be more effective in meeting daily challenges, responsibilities, and obligations in life.

"Each individual animal vibrates at a specific energy frequency, similar in principle to each person. The energy of each different species of animal is similar to that of a family: closely related, but remains separate. The energy of animals continually adapt to changes that occur within Nature, such as during the cycles of the four seasons.

"Animal behaviors show specific characteristics and abilities needed for survival. By getting to know these characteristics during each of the four seasons of the year, one will increase awareness, have a greater appreciation for their abilities, and learn more about the Laws of Nature. By learning about and becoming familiar with their routine patterns, humans may better understand the qualities needed for survival under all conditions and realize possible creative solutions that may result from each situation.

"Observation, contemplation, and realization from an objective higher perspective will help one see the interactions and patterns of all forms of life. When you take time to walk, you see and appreciate the smaller, more intricate moment-to-moment aspects of Nature. It is always best to experience Nature in person, but is not necessary. It is also possible to get wisdom from experiences of other people, from watching movies about wild animals, seeing domestic animals, and reading nature stories. One can learn many lessons when learning about all aspects of Nature. The enjoyment value is great, and the insights may be profound."

Frances: Animal Motivation, Survival

Francis paused, took a deep breath, and continued, "I love to speak about animals and insects. Today, I will give you an overview of their various motivations, such as, survival, adaptability, behaviors, body structures, and unique systems. Because I can speak about this information indefinitely, it will be a brief overview. Otherwise, we would be here for a very long time." We all laughed.

"Survival is at the root of all behavior for both animals and humans. All animals have a natural instinct that guides them throughout their lives. Their instinct controls their behavior, how they adapt to change, and what is necessary to do to survive. The character, or nature, of each animal may be similar, but all rely on their instincts.

"Humans have intuition instead of instinct to guide them during their life. However, humans may or may not follow their intuition. Free will and personal choice decide the eventual outcome of all circumstances. Intuition, though, is always available to follow or to change the course of any earlier decision."

"Each animal must live in the present moment because each moment may present new circumstances and challenges. Learning to live in the moment is one of the most important lessons for humans to learn from animal behavior. This awareness provides an opportunity to change one's life, to help one realize and be grateful for what one already has, and to slow down and appreciate and enjoy each moment.

"Thinking about the past or the future can distract from the value of the present moment. Continual regret of actions in the past brings sadness, depression, and anxiety. Dwelling on what one should or should not have done in the past results in regret, upset, and stress. This lowers the personal vibrational energy field, which may cause more regret, upset, and stress. Worrying about the future, over which one has no control, also may add to unnecessary stress and anxiety."

"A survival priority for both animals and humans is finding the necessities of life, such as food, water, and shelter. Finding food is a priority for all animals trying to survive. Some animals hunt at night while others during daylight hours. Some animals eat plants, nuts, and berries. Many are meat eaters who may hunt day and night. These animals are either predators or prey. However, even predators become prey to larger, more powerful animals.

"The abilities needed for survival include speed, agility, and a heightened sense of sight, smell, and hearing. Each plays a significant role in survival. Both predator and prey animals learn to take advantage of any opportunities that may help them survive. Both categories have different physical and behavioral traits and patterns.

"The predators are, by nature, better fighters and more aggressive. Their eyes are on the front of their face to focus on any movement from a prey animal in front of them. Their instinct is to kill smaller animals, and they usually have fewer offspring. The fox is a good example.

"The prey animals are, by nature, more cautious. They are always listening and are aware of their surroundings. Their eyes are on the side of their face to watch for any movement around them and looking for a fast escape route. They usually have many offspring. Mice are a good example.

"The female will nurse her young until they are ready to explore the outdoors. Either or both the male and female may bring food back to the nest, cave, or den until the young can find food on their own. Some animals mate for life, and also may share in the care of the young.

"Hunting is constantly being taught to the young. They may practice pouncing on each other in play. Ability and dominance, or leadership, over others is an essential lesson for them to learn before they become self-sufficient. Once mature, the young must leave the family unit. These young adult animals then find mates, set up their own nests, caves, or dens, and continue the cycle."

"Human nature and the changes that may occur during one's life may reflect the nature of animals when making necessary changes to survive, thrive, and possibly progress. The principles of survival, or survival techniques, may then apply to different conditions or circumstances in one's life.

"Some people enjoy working at night while others only during the day. There is a wide variety of types of employment, places to work, locations to live, and different benefit packages to help one consider the multitude of options and free will choices needed for survival and to enhance well-being.

"If one needs a change of action or a shift in perspective, observation of Nature's cycles may help. When seeing from a higher, more objective perspective, there is an expansion of one's conscious awareness, making one more open to new options and solutions to solve any number of problems. By observing the specific attributes of each animal and its abilities to survive, one can gain a greater understanding and awareness of traits, patterns, and flexibility. These attributes and abilities may then help show creative solutions as guidance and support for oneself and others in the ever-changing situations of life."

Francis: Animal Motivation, Adaptability

Once again, Francis paused and asked if I had questions yet. "Please feel free to ask anything whenever you think I'm going too fast, feel confused, or want a deeper explanation of something."

I took a deep breath and smiled. "Having always been interested in Nature, and especially animals of all kinds, this makes perfect sense. I never thought about the correlation between animals and humans. We always had pets growing up. I learned a lot about their behaviors, but have had little exposure to wild animals. This is interesting. I have no questions. Please continue."

"Okay. The second crucial survival trait for wild animals and humans is the ability to adapt to physical changes. Animals have an instinctive ability to adapt to changes in circumstances and weather conditions as they mature. By seeing the adaptation of animals, one may see the life lessons for humans. Let us use the change of seasons as an example.

"The fur of white-tail deer, foxes, and coyotes change under harsh winter conditions. It grows denser to keep the animal warm and protected from the elements. This winter layer, for some animals, is a different color to help blend them into the woods or the snow. The denser growth of the white-tail deer is a darker brown, similar to tree trunks. My favorite winter snow-time example is the weasel. In the summer, the fur of the weasel is brown with only a white throat and belly. In the winter, the fur is pure white in order to blend in with snow-covered areas. It is the same animal, but the name changes to Ermine.

"In summer, a lighter brown coat of fur replaces the dense dark fur of the white-tail deer to help them blend into their summer surroundings. The off-spring of many species have a temporary different colored fur to camouflage, protect, and hide them from predators. The brown fur with white spots of a fawn is a great example.

"By seeing how animals adapt to their changing conditions, humans learn to adapt to meet their challenges, responsibilities, and obligations of life. With expanded awareness, it is easier to adjust, overcome, and even take advantage of life situations as one matures and circumstances change.

"There are many examples of this, such as rules, regulations, laws, computer updates, procedures at work, loss of work, a new baby or grandchild, retirement, or maybe winning the lottery. Looking at all options to create solutions is an example of adapting to one's personal and/or professional life's conditions and circumstances.

"Here are some examples of human adaptability. A person moves to a warmer climate during the cold and snowy winter, or to a cooler climate during the hot summer. Or one moves into a community of like-minded people for support. Or one may take a new job closer to home or a job more aligned with personal goals. Lastly, one may increase the love and joy in one's life by getting more rest, by enjoying a new hobby, or joining a group to increase joyful activities in one's life. Change is beneficial when wanted or needed without fear and resistance."

Francis: Animal Motivation, Behavior

Francis sat down beside Benjamin and me under the shade of this oak tree. "There, that feels more comfortable. Any comments or questions?"

I shook my head back and forth. Francis nodded and continued speaking.

"Behavioral changes are the third most crucial survival trait for wild animals and humans. These changes may include hibernation in the winter for protection from severe weather conditions. One example is the black bear. Other animals may burrow into the ground and come out only when the weather is mild. An example is the chipmunk. Many species of birds migrate great distances to areas with a warmer or cooler climate to mate and have their young. These dependable cycles repeat every year.

"All animals, but especially personal pets, can show and teach us the greatest lesson of all - Unconditional Love. Personal pets show faith, trust, and loyalty. They can be constant friends and companions without judgment, criticism, or conditions. When people come home, their pets, especially dogs, will usually greet them with love and excitement. They reflect the love and attention given to them by their humans. Pets, such as seeing-eye dogs, work for us and ask for nothing in return. Most dogs will freely give their attention, loyalty, and love until they learn otherwise. Abuse and neglect by humans may change the personality of most pets.

"Pets remind us that there is a time for all things. They teach us that rest is essential. They show us it is important to laugh, love, and experience great joy by being playful. Cats are usually more independent than dogs, but quick to show their love when they feel your love. They purr and rub up against you and sometimes have loving expressions on their face. Mostly, personal pets show us how to enjoy every moment of every day."

"Humans also respond to love, kindness, consideration, and respect. They too will show their love when they feel love and often show love to strangers. Radiating love may continue for an entire lifetime or until he or she learns differently - by being physically abused, emotionally wounded, taken advantage of, deceived, abandoned, or unloved. If so, at some point in their life, he or she learns how to love again. Hopefully, he or she forgives themselves and others and continues to be the loving person they are.

"Each person can create needed change, solutions to problems, and see the possibility of even a small change, depending on different life circumstances. The observation of these motivational behaviors can inspire a new perspective of what may be possible to create a better living condition or a major change of employment.

"Do you have a favorite domestic or wild animal which gives you joy just thinking about it? Some people call this your totem animal. If you research the behavior and life patterns of this animal, you might find similarities between you and your totem animal. The patterns may give you insights into your behavioral patterns in your own life."

Francis: Animals and Insects, Physical Structures and Systems

Francis was still sitting in the lotus position under the mighty oak tree. He glanced over at me and said, "I will cover one more aspect of animals, which includes insects. Then we'll beam you back to Jacob at his residence. He was your first teacher/guide and will be the last. His wisdom is deep. He enjoys sharing, especially with students and those who are receptive, open, and understanding. Do you have any comments or questions so far?"

"No, only comments. I'm glad there's one more aspect about animals, but curious about the insects. Also, traveling on a beam of Light is incredible. I've experienced it twice and looking forward to a third time. It's amazing!"

"I agree with you and am pleased that you are pleased! Every part of every insect and animal has a function and a purpose. Observe the tiny intricacies and the many complexities of each body structure from the minute to the magnificent. Observe how each insect and animal finds food, shelter, and water. By knowing the function of each structure, it may be possible to learn the details of the life-cycle of any animal. By learning how they function and adapt to change in each of the four seasons, it may be possible to apply these tactics and traits to human life from a fresh, symbolic perspective.

"Do you realize that the aeronautics of birds and some insects, such as the dragonfly, helped to develop the airplane and the helicopter? We can learn much by examining the body structures of each type of insect and animal, from the small ant and spider to the enormous elephant and giraffe. Ants can carry ten to fifty times their body weight. Because they are so small, their muscles are thicker compared to their body size, unlike larger animals. Spiders have eight legs to help them move quickly, two body parts, and one antenna. They also have a silk-spinning organ at the end of their body. To add to that, they have a fang-like mouth part to kill the prey caught in their meticulously spun web. Elephants have a trunk used for smelling, eating grasses and fruits, breathing, trumpeting, digging for water and roots, drinking water, and spraying water over their body to stay cool. Giraffes are tall with a stretched spine, enabling them to feed on leaves high in the trees. Their spots help camouflage them and their long legs out run predators."

"Another concept to consider is that some insects have a programmed way of life. A colony of ants is an example of a distinctive system within the whole. There are many ants within each colony. Each ant has a specific job to perform for the welfare of the whole. The colony takes up a small area of ground but continues to get larger as the colony expands. Balance and harmony continue within the entire colony as long as each ant performs its programmed job properly. The colony is their entire world, with many lessons to be learned. The ants share and delegate duties with cooperation and compromise without conflict and resistance. None of the ants will ever know just how small they are and how vast the area is beyond their colony."

"Spiders are another example of a distinctive way of life. Their entire solitary world consists of the space of their web, which captures insects to consume for survival. The spider is tiny, yet able to spin a symmetrical and intricate web many times more massive than themselves. The silk-spinning organ exists within their bodies. It's fascinating to watch them spin their astonishingly beautiful webs. Do you think a spider knows the vastness of the world, or realizes there is a multitude of other animals and insects?"

"Let us now discuss the fish in the water and birds in the air. Each one lives in its own space to find food and survive. The larger the animal, the more area it needs to survive, such as goldfish versus the whale. Each survives and adapts differently according to its physical structure, characteristics, and patterns of adaptability. Each of these is subject to weather and water conditions, along with the space, or range, of area needed to survive. Each animal has no way of knowing about other animals, life forms, and struggles outside its own cycle of life."

"The last example is us, humankind. Humans are definitely the most complex animals on planet Earth. Each person thinks and reasons, makes easy decisions and tough choices, reacts violently or calmly responds, takes action or not, lives in balance and harmony, and acts out of love or fear. Humans have the entire Earth to live and learn on, share duties with or without cooperation and compromise, adapt to or resist change of life circumstances, and hopefully, enjoy life."

"There is an intricate detail of order, balance, and harmony within all systems of life on Earth - plant, animal and human. Do you think there might be a similar or higher system of life within the solar system or the Universe beyond? Do you think the Earth might be as tiny in the Universe as the ant is on Earth? Can you imagine the possibilities?

"These examples are observations of many things, but without detailed examination. The broader your perspective becomes, the more you realize, understand, and are able to adapt to circumstances in your life. By comparing animal and human behaviors and applying some of the instinctive survival qualities of the animals, humans may expand their awareness of options, free will, and choice. Changing behaviors and conditions in life may create more order, balance, and harmony. This will enhance confidence, safety, security, happiness, and a greater sense of well-being in their lives. When one applies the wisdom from the lessons learned from one's experiences, life becomes an adventure doing what one loves to do and also being of service to themselves and others in various capacities."

Francis paused, took a deep breath, and smiled at Benjamin and me. "That's all I have for you today. We hope that understanding these comparisons will help you use your imagination in new ways. As you delve deeper into each example, you will see the purpose of seeing beyond outer appearances.

"Humans are complex beings on many levels. Each person is on a different path, learning different lessons, and doing the best that he or she can do. Using the knowledge and wisdom gained so far, each person will find creative ways to change, survive, and thrive. He or she needs compassion, love, and forgiveness for themselves and others while enjoying one's journey in life. Finding purpose and meaning will open the heart and soul to know and feel the love of the Divine within."

I was speechless for a short time. Both of them looked at me lovingly. Finally, I responded. "Words are hard to express the amount of gratitude I have for both of you. You have changed my viewpoint of how to view Nature and life. I could never have imagined any of this before. Walking in the woods, or just being in Nature, I will never be the same again! Your comparisons are thought provoking. Some illustrations were easy to imagine, others took a little more thought before I could imagine it."

They both smiled and simultaneously said, "You are welcome!" And I laughed.

Benjamin continued, "It is our pleasure to meet you and to be of service. All the teachers/guides enjoy sharing our knowledge and wisdom. It is time for us to beam you back to Jacob. Remain seated there under this mighty oak tree. Close your eyes, and take as many deep breaths as necessary to relax your mind and body. Imagine being in that gorgeous garden where you first talked to Jacob. Feel the sun on your face, hear the chirping of the birds, and imagine sitting on that comfortable bench surrounded by beautiful flowers. Breathe normally and relax."

"May the pure Spirit and energy of God's creatures touch your heart and dwell in your soul."

~ FRANCIS ~

CHAPTER 8

The Final Wisdom of Jacob: Life Purpose and Ego

Relaxing there under the immense oak tree with my eyes closed felt wonderful. Birds were chirping and there was a gentle, warm breeze. Suddenly, there seemed to be a shift of energy and I could smell the scent of flowers. It jolted me out of my imagination. Opening my eyes, I was astonished once again. I was sitting there on that comfortable bench outside Jacob's house next to his gorgeous garden!

A few moments later, I saw Jacob standing off to my right, waiting for me to open my eyes. I was startled and jumped up. "Hello Jacob. I'm not sure if I'll ever get used to this mode of transportation, but I love it! Hopefully, learning how to beam myself from place to place is on my list of things to learn."

Jacob laughed and said, "All in good time, my dear. For now, though, have a seat and get comfortable. This will be your last session while here. At this time, there are things I would like to explain in more detail. Before we finish, you will have an opportunity to ask questions about life on Earth that we did not cover. Also, if there is anything you wish greater clarification of, please feel free to ask."

"That sounds wonderful, Jacob," I said. "This has been quite the experience. I am grateful for the information revealed so far. I will wait to ask questions until you finish. Please continue."

Jacob nodded and replied, "It pleases us that you wished for someone to talk with about your future. Your wish asked unseen forces for help, which turns out to be the Divine forces of God, Source Energy. 'Ask and you will receive' is another truth that many people don't remember or believe to be true. The answers are not always as literal as yours have been. Answers come in many ways, and is up to each person to listen, feel, and discern what happens after asking for help. We are just a thought away - as you are now aware of and happy about too!

"Having a life purpose applies to people everywhere, but circumstances in life are different for each person. One may feel a life purpose as a burning desire that must be done, but not understood. Raising one's vibrational frequency and consciously connecting the Physical and Spirit Realms, can align one with spirit guides. This allows he or she to receive knowledge and understanding while living in the Physical Realm.

"Some people receive an inspirational idea and follow through with actions to carry out that inspiration. Some people believe they have no life purpose and think that there is something wrong. Have faith and trust that just being yourself is enough. Some people radiate Light to all people they come into contact with, but don't realize it.

The soul brings to itself whatever is necessary to fulfill its blueprint for living in the physical world. Unknown opportunities may present themselves. Each person has a life purpose, but it may not be what was thought or could ever have imagined.

"Each person in the Physical Realm vibrates at a slightly different level, or vibrational frequency, resulting in varying degrees of consciousness. Each person, with intention, can shift energies to a higher vibration to increase spiritual awareness and higher consciousness. In other words, all people can connect with the two realities and even to God. Remember, the thinking mind is the connector between the intellectual and the inspirational, making this possible at any time."

"The ego-mind is part of the thinking mind, the intellectual mind, and is called the Ego. The ego-mind bases its thoughts and opinions on past experiences, decisions, and choices within the current lifetime. It knows how he or she negatively judged them at the time. The ego tries to protect the person from repeating earlier mistakes. The ego also assumes that decisions will remain negative and that he or she will fail at any attempt to do something new or in a different way. It is the little voice in the head that says things like "No, you can't", "You've never done that before", "What will you do if something goes wrong?", "Who do you think you are to even try this?". The little voice judges the past trying to protect the future from failure.

"Another purpose of the ego-mind is to trigger a negative emotional reaction to a thought, word, or deed which makes no sense at the time. A trigger can originate from a friend, family member, a stranger, or even a news program. Any triggered reaction results from a past emotional wound or trauma. The trigger is a clue to a negative emotion trapped somewhere in the body that needs to be released. When this happens, a deep analysis of past personal experiences is warranted to discover why the trigger occurred. One must ask one's self questions to remember experiences with similar reactions and feelings. He or she must ask 'why' questions until a pattern of behavior and the root cause is discovered. This is the point of pain from the original wound or trauma that is still causing the same negative emotional reaction.

"Once the root cause is known, a deep understanding and healing takes place. Other similar patterns may continue to surface, which reinforce the understanding. When future experiences trigger the same reaction, one will recognize the pattern, have an 'ah-ha' moment, and avoid the negative pattern. Instead, the response can be more positive or neutral to the situation.

"The ego-mind indirectly causes this deep self-analysis, which expands the conscious awareness of one's self, of projections toward others, and of personal expectations of self and others in many situations. It also causes each person to be still, to think, and to realize what is important. It helps one decide if he or she is ready to make changes to move toward dreams and desires. It helps one see options, solutions, and the need for strong boundaries. Most importantly, the ego-mind ultimately makes positive changes helping one learn from past mistakes without judgement or criticism, and trying new things without fear of failure. Once one takes control and responsibility of one's life, the influence of the ego-mind will be less prominent when making decisions, or not involved at all. The ego contrasts the negatively judged past experiences with the positive, heart-centered dreams and desires of the future.

"It may take many years before one realizes the role of the ego in one's life. The ego helps each person grow beyond the human self, finding the deeper path to one's soul, which is the Light within, the real-self, the consciousness aligned with the soul's purpose for being here. The ego is a blessing in disguise. Having greater awareness, one realizes how powerful, confident, worthy, and responsible one is for all personal choices and decisions. Experiences become more positive each time one ignores the opinions of the ego in favor of the inspirations of the heart and soul, bringing one closer to dreams and desires.

"The ego is there for a reason. It too is Divine and is to be loved and cherished as a messenger of God, who prods each person to go deeper and deeper within. This helps each person recognize and release trapped emotional blockages with ease and grace. Then high vibrational energies of Divine Love and Light enter, replacing the released blockages. With each release, one travels the path back home to the soul and to God through our consciousness. The result is peace, love, and joy within the heart and soul!"

"The soul is eternal and knows one's past-life experiences. The soul knows the reason one returns to earth, the present-day blueprint for this lifetime, and sees all possibilities for the future. It fills each person with Divine Love to encourage one to try new things, go to new places, meet new people, and experience life to the fullest with peace, love, joy, and abundance of all things. The inspiration that one feels is leading to one's dreams and desires. The soul brings opportunities to each person so he or she learns the lessons intended for this lifetime. However, there is free will and choice to accept these opportunities or not. Some people view the opportunities as obstacles or problems, but each opportunity is a blessing in disguise. Once the lesson is truly learned, the resulting wisdom integrates and is applied.

"Life changes and priorities change, too. There becomes a balance between the physical ego-mind and the spiritual love-filled heart. When there is an awareness of the limitless Unconditional Love in both realms, it is easier to open one's heart. After making a soul connection with God, the Divine, one feels these higher vibrational energies.

"Once this occurs, one is receptive to the limitless love, peace, power, strength, wisdom, and guidance available from all levels in all dimensions at any time. With increased knowledge, understanding, and conscious aware-ness, one realizes greater balance and harmony in life. He or she begins to believe how important, worthy, and deserving he or she is to have personal needs and desires satisfied. Eventually, one is in complete control of personal thoughts, feelings, words, and actions. Being filled with happiness leads to the life of one's dreams."

Jacob paused, looked at me, and commented, "You look confused. Are you okay? Do you understand this concept of mind, ego-mind, and soul?"

"Oh my goodness, Jacob." I responded. "I had such a terrible opinion of the Ego! My belief was that it was my worst enemy, always trying to trip me up with many things I tried to do. I understand the flow of energy between the mind and the soul, but I never attached the Ego with anything positive. To think of it as God's way to help us analyze and rethink our choices toward our future is completely new to me. Superficial materialistic choices seem easy, but soul-level choices about our future are more difficult, even scary. That's probably why so many people are more comfortable in the materialistic world. Looking deep into one's self reveals many things that people would rather ignore or be in denial of, myself included if I'm being honest about this.

"The fact that the soul draws opportunities to us for our benefit is also something that never occurred to me. I will definitely be more aware of and listen to my thoughts and examine my beliefs and expectations about many things. I'll also try to think of problems as opportunities, but that is more of a challenge. This information is amazing and thought-provoking. Wow!"

Jacob: Doorways and Energy Centers

Jacob smiled at me and said, "It pleases us that you understand the importance of self-analysis, and the healing of old wounds and traumas. Recognizing, understanding, and releasing old wounds allows more Divine Light to enter the soul and raise the vibrational frequency."

After feeling the truth of these revelations, I excitedly said, "For me, this information answers big questions. I will view my life differently from now on. Though I'm still in shock to hear that the Ego is a blessing in disguise!"

"Yes, that can be shocking to many. There are different beliefs and perspectives about the Ego, each depending on different philosophies. I am pleased that you understand the deeper meaning. If you are ready to continue, I will quickly review more of this information. I know we discussed it earlier, but I want you to realize how important it is to understand and integrate the conscious awareness of your thoughts and, especially, beliefs about yourself, choices you make, and what actions you take."

I nodded, and he continued speaking. "There are doorways between the physical and spiritual worlds. Doorways stand for a transformation of energy. All beings at the same frequency can see one another just as easily as you see each other in the third dimension. We cannot see other people at different frequencies, or levels, until there is a shift to that frequency. It is the same principle as not being able to listen to more than one radio station. One must change the frequency before one hears another station.

"Beings from all levels can shift their vibrational frequency, transform their energy, and adjust their frequency to another higher or lower level, including the Physical Realm. The transformation to higher frequencies also includes shifts in time and space. The Physical Realm is a low frequency. The Celestial Realm is one of the highest.

"Occasionally, spirits may physically appear in the physical world by shifting their energy field to a dense, lower frequency. Beings in the angelic realm often do this to help in emergency situations. When the energy field of physical spirits or angels return to their higher frequency in the Spirit Realm, they seem to disappear.

"A doorway to transformation can be physical, mental, or spiritual. Each time one shifts one's vibration or frequency, it becomes easier to feel the subtle differences within the energy field on each level. Ultimately, one becomes more aware of the limitless possibilities for each day and for the future.

"There is a scientific explanation for everything that happens in the Universe. The earlier examples involving time, space, cycles, systems, vibration, frequency, dimensions, and alternate realities all follow the Natural Laws of the Universe, also called Universal Laws. You can learn about these laws, based on scientific principles, if you desire. When we reach the highest realm, all mysteries are revealed.

"Each lesson one learns in life increases vibrational frequency, conscious awareness, and advances the soul on the path to enlightenment, perfection, and joy. It is vitally important to realize that choices made, and actions taken within each lifetime, decide future possibilities for one's life and one's soul. As conscious awareness increases, one's sense of responsibility increases to control one's thoughts, feelings, and well-being. There are unlimited opportunities to make changes in one's life and to advance the soul. The knowledge, skills, and abilities one earns in each lifetime remain part of one's soul and influence one's personality and character.

"You are the same soul at all times, forever. The soul never dies. The soul continues to learn in the Spirit Realm and continues to express that learning with actions in the Physical Realm. When one learns lessons in each consecutive lifetime, there is greater knowledge and understanding of life, greater personal power, conscious awareness, and ultimately, soul evolution. The evolution of the soul is a cycle between the two realms.

"Each accomplishment will increase the individual's power and vibrational frequency. The rewards are health, happiness, love, peace, joy, abundance, power, prosperity, strength, spiritual evolution, and ultimately, the perfection of the soul."

"Understanding this information is vital to one's eternal soul and to all future lifetimes. Once one learns this soul-level knowledge, it stays in the subconscious mind from lifetime to lifetime. Sometimes one experiences this soul knowledge as an inner knowing of things not yet learned in the present lifetime. A few examples are having strong emotions, good and bad, about different countries and cultures in the world; along with a preference for food, music, and traditions. There may also be unexplained higher personal standards with deep convictions and emotions about many moral and ethical issues for no obvious reason, even at a young age.

"The doorway to transformation is to be objective and neutral in many situations without judgment or criticism of yourself and others. When in doubt, it is best to take a moment and see any situation from a higher vibrational viewpoint. From there, one can be more objective and perceive the higher, broader perspectives, the bigger picture, and see the lesson for all involved. One may perceive any situation as good or bad, right or wrong, great or small. However, wisdom is learned and integrated from every situation."

I looked over at Jacob after concentrating on what he was explaining. "Yes, I did not realize the full impact of the importance of learning lessons and integrating the wisdom into my life. It is now, and I will remember it, especially in difficult situations. It amazes me how everything affects everything else in life. It's mind-boggling! Even the smallest acts of kindness or prayers for others, makes a difference in the lives of so many people."

Jacob laughed and nodded. "Yes, and there is more. Unconditional Love is next."

Jacob: Unconditional Love in the Spirit Realm

"God's Unconditional Love permeates throughout all levels and can be felt and remembered by all souls at a deep level. Unconditional Love in the Spirit Realm is comparable to oxygen in the Physical Realm - as you experienced when we first met and traveled to a higher dimension.

"While living in the physical world, each person may search for something of meaning, but be unaware of what that might be. During different times in life, each person may feel one's life is stuck in a rut or feel alone, even when surrounded by people. Many may feel this as an empty void in one's life. It doesn't seem to matter how much money is earned, what social status is achieved, how many possessions one owns, or how much power and control one believes they have.

"This search for meaning in life occurs because the soul and the subconscious mind remember the Spirit Realm and the different higher energies found there. Unconditional Love is the strongest and permeates all things and all places on all levels. Physical life becomes an unconscious search, and maybe even a struggle, to obtain and feel these energies again, but especially Unconditional Love.

"The need for Love becomes the motivation and driving force during all of physical life, whether or not recognized. Each person makes decisions and choices based on this unconscious need. Each person's life revolves around everything one loves - decorating the home, eating favorite foods, enjoying hobbies, chosen professions, and even joining organizations. Other examples may include watching or taking part in athletics, listening to certain types of music, watching movies, having a pet, and being in Nature. The most important of all is loving relationships. Each decision depends on the amount of happiness, love, and joy received from each of these, and many others, to increase the amount of love felt in one's life. Having a pet is a wonderful example, especially cats and dogs. Our beloved pets mirror back to us pure unconditional love no matter what and without conditions.

"Eventually, there is a choice in life between the physical, materialistic world and the spiritual, Divine love-filled world. Both paths are always present, but one path eventually becomes dominant in one's life. If one chooses the spiritual path, there is an awakening to a more significant meaning in one's life with faith and trust. Many blessings already present in life become clearer and more realized with gratitude. If one chooses the physical, materialistic path, life continues, but there may be a deeper longing to find the love and meaning to one's life."

Jacob glanced at me and said, "Understanding Unconditional Love is important too, but not as difficult to understand. The next subject may be a little challenging. It is connecting to the Universal Forces of God. I will continue if you don't have any questions or comments."

I nodded my head and said with excitement, "Wow. Learning how to make that connection sounds amazing, Jacob. I get thoughts of inspiration, but consciously connecting would be life-changing!"

Jacob: Universal Forces of God with a Meditation

"Yes, making that connection can change one's life and may be easier than you think," Jacob commented, and took a deep breath before continuing. "Every man, woman, and child can communicate with God, the Divine. All things are of God and from God expressing through humanity. Each person is a child of God, with the spark of life within the heart connected to the soul. Each person is on a journey in life to increase conscious awareness of this connection to the Divine within, ultimately perfecting the soul and becoming a conduit of God's grace, love, blessings, and forgiveness for others struggling in the Physical Realm.

"God expresses love for humanity in each person through love and concern for others. God's way to perfection is through balance, harmony, power, strength, wisdom, joy, and, especially, Love. The Physical Realm is often the hard way, but life was never meant to be hard. Duality and polarity in the third-dimension present many challenges to be overcome on the path back to the Divine. That is the journey of life.

"With the help of the Ego, one learns the triggers, the cause of negative emotional reactions. Deep self-analysis that delves into past traumatic experiences helps one to remember, recognize, and release the root cause of the current trigger with love, compassion, and forgiveness for themselves and others. Often, when young, he or she creates judgements or misunderstandings about themselves and others without full knowledge of the situation. With each release, there is an increase in conscious awareness. As consciousness expands, one becomes more aware of the unseen Universal Forces of the Divine, which helps one integrate the wisdom one learns from the release of each triggered experience.

"The connection to the Divine within is the source of power for the limitless Universal Forces. When one consciously makes that connection and allows the Love of God to pour through them, one realizes the limitless abilities of the mind. One also realizes the potential to visualize, idealize, conceive, and bring forth what one needs, all in Divine timing. The physical self can express God's perfection through the personality with thought, words, feelings, and actions. One can also radiate that Love out to all beings. With clarity, patience, and courage, changes occur to help create a happier, more fulfilled life."

Jacob paused for a moment, looked at me again, and continued. "This is a short meditation to connect to God and the Universal Forces. It can be changed to fit your daily needs in whatever way feels most comfortable."

Meditation

"Stand up, move around, and stretch your body to release your tight muscles. Then sit down and get comfortable. Take a deep breath and hold. Exhale and sigh out loud to release any tension. Quiet the mind, and become silent. Your eyes may be open or closed, whichever you prefer. Relax and breathe deeply several times. With each breath, let go of the stress or trauma of the day. Breathe normally. Breathe in and feel peace. Breathe out stress and feel your body letting go. Inhale peace. Exhale and relax. Inhale peace. Exhale and relax. Silence the mental chatter. Empty your mind. Slowly, relax your jaw, your shoulders, and every muscle in your body. Keep relaxing into the silence. Allow your breath to slow down and relax. Breathe in peace. Breathe out and relax. (Pause)

"Feel the beating of your heart. Feel the rhythm of your heartbeat. Visualize the center of your heart. See a beautiful doorway. It is the doorway to your soul in the center of your heart. How does it look? Open the door and walk through it. Enter a large, beautiful room with humble gratitude. You appear to be alone in this room. Look around. How is it decorated? What do the walls look like? Are there crystals? What colors do you see? Do you smell anything? In the center of the room, there is a large chair that looks like a throne. Walk to it. Touch it and then sit down. How does your throne make you feel? Can you feel the power and connection with your soul? Relax and quiet your mind. (Pause)

"Within the silence, know that the Divine hears you. Search your heart for emotional love. Think of and feel the happiest moment of your life that fills you with the greatest love you've ever felt. It could be your first kiss, the day you were married, the day you held your first baby, playing with your pet, or watching a magical sunset. In your mind's eye, see, experience, and feel your greatest love. Feel the power of that love within you.

"Know that it is Unconditional Love in your heart and is the seat of the soul. See the spark of Divine White Light within, the connection to God, the Divine. Take your time. Visualize the White Light expanding outward from your heart with each breath. Align your whole being with the Divine Light within your heart and soul. Feel your body getting lighter and lighter. Feel this energy filling every cell and empty space of your body and then expanding to surround you like a cocoon. Fill your being with that blissful Unconditional Love until your body is completely immersed in and surrounded by it.

Take your time. You will become sensitive and receptive to the subtle energies found in and around you - now within the Spirit Realm.

"Keep breathing normally and stay relaxed.

"Know you are in the presence of God, your guides, and your spiritual teachers.

"When you sense this higher connection, talk to God with a sincere heart.

"Visualize and feel the emotion of whatever you want to discuss. Talk to God silently or out loud, whichever feels the best for you, until everything is expressed. Ask any questions you may have to better understand circumstances on your path of life. Feel deeply the emotion of the needed desire. Ask for knowledge and understanding of the Truth of all things. Ask to see things as God sees them.

"Pause for a few minutes or as long as you need after each subject or question. Then feel the emotion of the granted desire as it takes place.

"When finished, express thankfulness, gratitude, and appreciation.

"Your guides and spiritual teachers will leave as you slowly return to ordinary consciousness. Take as much time as needed. When ready, take a few deep breaths. Then gently wiggle your fingers and feet. Slowly open your eyes. Record any messages received, anything that you saw, were told, or was done - before you forget them.

"Practice this meditation as much as you like. Once you become familiar with the process, you'll be able to access the Divine quickly. All Divine beings are just one thought away."

It took me a few minutes to come back to ordinary consciousness. "Oh, my goodness! This meditation will help me and many others. I am so happy, even thrilled, to have this opportunity to ask questions and get explanations whenever I feel the need to do so. I am so grateful that you intervened in my life and appreciate each of you for explaining, 'Who are we?' and 'Why are we here?' and 'Why are things the way they are?' and especially, 'What is God's Truth?' However, I do have two more questions: "Why are you giving me all this amazing information?" and, "Does everyone coming here receive this time, attention, and all the insights of both the Physical and Spirit Realms?"

Jacob's Reason for Giving This Information

Jacob, with a serious tone in his voice, answered my question. "Yes, we reveal the insights of both realms to anyone searching for truth at the level that one can understand. It is essential that you know and understand all of these examples. We freely give this information to all who search for truth. For you, Sharon, it was in response to your wish for someone to talk with about your thoughts of suicide. Our wish, purpose, and hope was that the information revealed would help answer questions, increase awareness of both realms, and influence your choice enough to remain in the physical world.

"For everyone else, we give this information to help reduce the fear of death, to convince them that they are part of a much grander plan, that each life is unique, essential, and connected to God. Hopefully, this information also helps everyone realize that God's unconditional faith, hope, and love genuinely exist, and is accessible to all souls everywhere in all realms at all times.

"This information is an incentive to help individuals become better people for themselves and for all of humanity. It also reassures everyone that they make a difference with every good thought, word, and deed, no matter how small, even if there is no apparent recognition of it. Finally, this information helps people to know and realize the importance of their ability to pursue and achieve the dreams and desires that give their life passion, purpose, and meaning, along with the growth of their soul.

"However, it is also important to persevere with conviction and commitment to continue on that path, even during the many tough times that may occur. Remember, the tough times are the stepping stones to learning life lessons on the way of attaining the goal. Think of the detours as opportunities to gain experience and also to bring out and advance the hidden strengths and abilities you never thought you had. This is the journey we are all on, whether realized or not."

"The mission of life is to have a personal connection with God, to be loving, kind, joyful, gentle, patient, respectful to all, have fun, enjoy life, and see and learn lessons from all forms of life."

"The mission of the soul is to learn compassion, love, and forgiveness for yourself and others, to strive for perfection, and lastly, to refine, heal, and purify your soul. Also, to know that there is meaning in all thoughts and actions working toward a higher purpose. As a result, each person will reap the benefits of soul growth in more ways than anyone could ever imagine in the present lifetime and in each progressive lifetime."

"The ultimate purpose, the final goal of life and our soul, is to reach the highest level of the Spirit Realm, to experience pure Divine Love, Peace, and Joy, and be able to stay there forevermore. We do this by going through that Doorway of Transformation as many times as necessary, lifetime after lifetime, until we perfect our soul."

"It gives me, and all of us here in the Spirit Realm, great pleasure to have this opportunity to be of service. We hope this helps give you a greater understanding of why it is important to change your decision about taking an early exit from planet Earth. For everyone else who becomes aware of this information, we hope it affects your life, helps you understand how powerful you are, and that you have influence in your world, and can possibly influence others."

Jacob paused for a moment and smiled. "Please remember - trust your loving inner voice and intuition. Also, God is and we are just a thought away for help."

I excitedly added, "I remember seeing a picture of a sunrise over the ocean in my chiropractor's office with a quote at the bottom. The meaning of it now, for me, is more profound than ever. The quote is:

"We never know how far-reaching something we may Think, Say, or Do today...will affect the lives of millions tomorrow."

BY B. J. PALMER, D.C. PH.C.

"Thank you, Jacob and all the others, from the bottom of my heart, for this knowledge and for the many truths in both realms. I will never consider ending my life again, thanks to all of you and your revelations. Everything has changed for me now and for my future. My love, gratitude, and appreciation for each of you are beyond measure!"

"Until we meet again ~
May your journey be filled with God's Grace, Love, Light,
and Infinite Blessings, Always."

~ Jacob ~

PART TWO

Personal Stories

These are personal stories that happened before and after the Divine Intervention, which I believe confirm much of the information and wisdom revealed in Part One.

Looking back on my life, I realize that my personal experiences and abilities felt normal to me, and wrongly assumed everyone had similar experiences. There were lucid dreams and out-of-body experiences which I mostly thought were bizarre dreams until later in life. Mystical, unseen experiences, rooted in my unconscious, intrigued me the most. Each one held the promise of additional insights into my soul and my life while living here on Earth. The following are events that helped clarify my thoughts, beliefs, and emotions; along with confirmation of the information revealed in Part One.

Every day can become an astonishing adventure!

#1

Reaction to War

Before my teenage years in the early 1960s, my family would watch documentaries of original films of World Wars I and II. Watching men die senseless deaths was heartbreaking for me. I would get furious at the leaders of each country for their lack of maturity to solve their problems. Thousands of people were affected by war because of their egos and hunger for power and control. Battles raged on. Thousands of soldiers and civilians lost their lives on both sides. Cities were destroyed over ownership of land that actually belongs to our beloved Mother Earth. My parents never said much about my outbursts. They looked at me like I was just too young to understand how the world really worked. They ignored and sometimes smiled at my comments. I would then get more upset, not understanding why they didn't see and feel how wrong the killing was - the same way I did.

Later, in my early twenties, I had a recurrent dream about a German soldier during World War II, who was about the same age that I was at the time of the dream. As I recall the dream, it was wartime, and I was seeing a destroyed city in Germany. There were large stone buildings, but mostly rubble, with an occasional corner or two still standing. There was a young German soldier alone hiding behind one of these corners, carefully looking around in all directions, nervously clutching his gun. I looked in the direction he was focusing on and saw American forces marching down the middle of what used to be a large street. There were foot soldiers armed with machine guns in front of and around the sides of three large tanks. The German soldier tried to hide, but as the Americans got closer, they saw him, shot him, and killed him - just because he was a German soldier. It was wartime, and I now understand that you kill or be killed during a war. However, the principle of a conflict that caused so many innocent people to die is what bothered me the most, and still does.

After having this dream multiple times, a friend suggested I see a psychic medium in a nearby city to possibly learn the meaning of the dream. I made an appointment. The psychic's name was Ann. It didn't take long after I described my dream and how emotional I felt about it, that Ann had an answer. She looked at me and asked if I believed in reincarnation. I said, "Yes, I do now," but never told her about the Divine Intervention at nineteen.

Ann absolutely amazed me by saying the soldier in the dream was me in my last lifetime! The trauma of having been killed was so strong that I recalled the memory in my subconscious mind during this lifetime. She explained a few other details. It shocked me, but I believed her. This information felt true deep within my heart and soul. It stunned me when Ann said that since I now know and understand this information, I probably would never dream about it again.

She was correct. I never had that dream again. Ann's interpretation of the dream explained many things about my feelings and reactions to the cruelty of any war. Most things that violate principles of life and integrity still bring out a strong, opinionated side of my personality. Whenever I focus on being that German soldier in a different lifetime during World War II, long-forgotten memories come flooding back, both good and bad.

The memory of that dream surfaces with every discussion about violence, war, destruction, and senseless killing. However, now I keep my opinions to myself and say a prayer for peace with compassion, love, and forgiveness for all involved. Thankfully, I now believe that when experiences trigger past-life memories, it confirms my belief in reincarnation, in cycles of lifetimes, in the higher perspective of life lessons, and in the fact that anything is possible.

#2

Dream within a Spaceship

While a teenager, I would receive visions or insights, mostly in dreams, and go to the library to research the possibilities. One night while in high school, I dreamt I was in a spaceship, being shown around by a person who looked much like a human. The metal covering the walls was not familiar to me. I was told the ship ran on electromagnetic energy and this metal functioned as a storage battery. The name of the metal was never mentioned. I wish I had asked many questions - like I usually do.

It was hard for me to imagine how the walls could hold electromagnetic energy like a battery, and then, how could the energy be integrated into the spaceship's working power. It was a mystery to me.

That dream prodded me to the library once again to research electromagnetic energy. I was still a young teenager and unable to understand the math and science behind this concept. My mind could not comprehend it and thought it probably would take an electrical engineer to understand it. I asked several people questions about the subject, but told no one why I was asking.

Some of the other walls on the spaceship appeared to be made of something that looked like gold. There was continuous writing on them in vertical rows from floor to ceiling. The writing looked familiar and reminded me of Egyptian hieroglyphics that I had seen on a television show, but yet it was different. I didn't know what it said, and the person showing me around didn't mention the meaning of any of the writings. Now occasionally, when in meditation, I

101

see a gold wall covered with writing on it in vertical rows. It reminds me of that experience years ago, but I still do not know what the meaning is of the writing on the gold walls.

#3

Vision of a Solar ATV

While a young teenager, I received a vision of what looked like an all terrain vehicle. It reminded me of a snowmobile, except it was no ordinary snowmobile. This machine was more of a Land Rover, but the same size as a snowmobile or a riding lawnmower. The shape of it was like a massive egg with the narrow end to the front. Attached to the outside of the machine were small solar panels. It had a solar battery back-up to start the engine and to store any excess energy. Ordinary daylight would supply enough energy for it to run during the day. Excess energy in the battery was sufficient for nighttime traveling. There were no fossil fuels needed at all. The model I saw in the vision would seat two people side-by-side. It looked like an airplane cockpit, complete with a clear shield over the cockpit to cover their heads and to protect them from the elements.

However, the most fantastic thing about this solar machine was that there were interchangeable attachments to put on the bottom. There were snow skis, wheels with all-weather tires, flat traction wheels like tanks, and even something like small pontoons similar to what airplanes use for take-off and landing on water. This solar machine was an authentic all-terrain vehicle for personal use in all weather conditions.

Once attending college, I tried to get a couple of engineering students to build it as a project, but they quickly dismissed my unrealistic fantasy. Thinking about it now, I'm not surprised. It was over 40 years ago, and the use of solar energy was just becoming known. It has taken years for solar power technology to be perfected and now to be used in many areas of life on earth.

Later in life, I received a message that it was okay to abandon the project. Since I believed it would be an impressive vehicle, I wondered why. My first thought was that, the kind soul who originally sent me the vision, realized I was not capable of building it on my own or to have this machine built. A second thought was that someone else had the good fortune to receive the same vision and has actually built it. At least I hope so. I keep looking for it. Anything is possible!

#4

Observing a Galactic Federation Meeting

While in high school, my interests and feelings differed from most of the other students. However, I wanted to fit in and belong, and did my best to do that. No one knew about my empathic nature, my innermost feelings, and how I could feel other's emotional pain. I also didn't feel comfortable telling anyone about it. As usual, I became very good at stuffing down my true emotions; mostly the sadness, hurts, and disappointments of my many unrealistic expectations.

At the same time, I enjoyed having fun with friends and usually kept busy. At night, I would continue to have dreams of unknown places with people I never met. Sometimes, the dreams felt so real I wasn't sure if it had happened or not.

On a couple of occasions, I dreamt I was observing a meeting. In one of these dreams, there was a large rectangular table with twelve people seated around it. Each person looked physically different from the others. Some looked much different from humans. I sat at one end of the table beside a man I assumed to have been my guide. There was no fear of being with him even though I did not know where we were.

A man at the other end of the table stood up and looked around at the others talking amongst themselves. He waited until it was quiet. He was holding a small piece of wood, which looked like a judge's gavel. He hit the table with it three times and said, "I now bring this meeting of the Galactic Federation to order!"

I gasped and everyone turned to look at me. It surprised them to see a young girl from Earth who had no business sitting at the table with representatives from other planets. The man that was with me quickly told them not to worry. It was okay that I was there, and that I was just observing for now. Then everything went blank, and I woke up. That's another vision I will never forget!

#5

My Divine Intervention

At nineteen, I secretly planned my suicide. It was my first semester of college, and I was having second thoughts. My empathic heart had gotten the best of me. I decided life was too hard and wanted to go back to my spiritual home. I had many questions, wished that I had someone to talk with, and ultimately, asked for guidance.

Much to my surprise, a spiritual being, who I believed to be one of my guides, came that night in my dream state and showed me the Other-Side of life. He explained many things to me, so that I could make more of an informed decision about ending my life. My guide talked about life, death, and our connection to the Divine. He also explained the purpose and meaning of why things are the way they are here on Earth and also in the spirit world.

My life changed profoundly that night, and the experience has helped to expand my conscious awareness every day since. The information that has been revealed is the reason for writing this book, along with the desire to share this wisdom.

After realizing how precious life is and deciding that I would never contemplate suicide again, I began reading and researching beliefs, philosophies, and religions. The list included religious beliefs, mystical stories, reincarnation, out-of-body experiences, near-death experiences, psychics, and mediums. Also, I studied energy healing from various modalities; such as Reiki, Integrated Energy Healing, Reconnection, Tai Chi, yoga, acupuncture, acupressure, and others. Reading and learning information about these sub-jects became my favorite thing to do for years. See Part One for the full story.

#6

Edgar Cayce and the A.R.E.

In my search for spiritual information, I learned about Edgar Cayce and the Association of Realization and Enlightenment (A.R.E.) in Virginia Beach, Virginia. Becoming a member allowed me to borrow as many as I wanted of his 4,000 readings transcribed or recorded while in a trance. I learned more than I could ever have imagined. People considered him a sleeping prophet because he answered questions and gave helpful advice while appearing to be asleep. He was actually in a trance state-of-mind. Many have written books over the years about Edgar Cayce. His readings included medical treatments for various health conditions, along with insightful information on other topics all given through him while he was in an unconscious trance.

The A.R.E. is still in Virginia Beach, Virginia. Today, it has a library and catalog of his readings, along with current classes and presentations. Edgar Cayce's information confirmed things that my guide told me on that fateful intervention night which applies to everyone. The list includes reincarnation, telepathy, receiving inspirational messages, mental downloads and concepts, and visitations from souls, or spirits, on the Other Side.

Each of these help increase our conscious awareness, understanding, and consciousness of many things about life; such as relationships, our life purpose, and being of service to others. However, these topics are not taught in school, and I was grateful to learn more about each of them from the Association of Realization and Enlightenment, the A.R.E.

Most of all, I am very grateful to realize that the "intervention dream" was not just a dream after all.

#7

Channeling with Confirmations

One of the many books that I read in my search for spiritual information was called *Soul Sounds* by Mary Summer Rain. It was her first book in a series of more to come. The stories included her experiences as she learned the ways of Native American traditions. She opened my eyes and my heart to a whole new level of conscious awareness, along with understanding the limitless possibilities of our mind, body, and soul.

It was exciting every time she released a new book in her series. I was anxious to see what would be discussed, and what else I could learn that would light up my life. In one of her books, there was a section saying that if the reader had any questions or comments, to write to Mary Summer Rain. My mind was spinning! I sat down with pen and paper to formulate my many questions. In the end, there were a total of ten questions.

An astonishing thing happened. With each and every question I wrote out in the letter, thoughts appeared in my head, answering my question. After every question, I either heard thoughts, saw a mental vision, or received a mental download of a complete concept. All questions were answered and explained in detail. I was flabbergasted, was so happy, and smiled all evening. I never sent the letter!

Looking back on that day, I realize it was my first experience of channeling information from unseen sources, but I was not aware of what that was at the time. Channeling information was rarely discussed. Many people were skeptical about believing anything channeled, and are still skeptical today. The readings by Edgar Cayce were all documented with proof. He had trance-channeled thousands of times to help emotionally and physically heal many people. My experience seemed completely different. I was thrilled, but told no one. I convinced myself that no one would believe me, and that everyone would think that I made it up. So, once again, silence became my friend.

After that first channeling experience, I would sometimes mentally ask my unseen friend, or friends, for help. If I had a question or needed more information, I would become still, stop the chatter in my mind, and then focus on my question. After I asked it, I would patiently listen. Within a minute, I would usually receive a mental thought or a vision. The response would be a yes or no, with or without requested information. The answers were not necessarily what I wanted to hear, but were answers I needed to hear for my own good.

One example of receiving channeling confirmation happened years later. I was looking for a large, thick, and heavy Sears Roebuck catalog for several days. I searched the house several times. It surprised me because it was a small house, and the catalog was very large. The next day, while driving home from work, I asked out loud, "Where is that catalog?" I did not expect any response. But instantly, I heard, "It's on top of the bookcase under a plant!" Wow, was I surprised and excited to check that spot.

When I arrived home, and before I checked for the catalog, I told a friend at the house what had happened so there would be a witness. My only bookcase was tall, with a two-inch wood trim around the top and an ivy plant trailing down the side. After finding my step stool, I climbed up, lifted the pot, and laughed out loud. There it was! My large, thick, heavy Sears Roebuck catalog was under the plant raising it up to see the plant better! I had forgotten all about putting the catalog up there. My friend and I both laughed and thanked my unseen friend. Gratitude, love, and joy filled my being!

Several years later, I experienced another channeling confirmation. Sometimes, I questioned if the channeling was really happening. One night while driving home from work, I had a mental conversation with my unseen friends, asking for confirmation. I listed the reasons why I was questioning and then apologized for asking for confirmation. Knowing that they could do or arrange anything, I asked for what I thought was an impossible task. If it really happened, I would know I wasn't crazy.

At the time, I worked the evening shift at a nearby hospital lab, getting out of work at midnight. It took forty-five minutes to get home, and I always listened to the radio on the way. One of my favorite songs was two years old, but I hadn't heard it played for a long time. So, I asked my unseen friends to have the song "Keeper of the Stars" by Tracy Byrd, played the next night at 12:30 a.m.. I'm a sappy, die-hard romantic in love with Love. This song was one of my favorites. Again, I told no one about this preposterous request.

The next night, my unusual request filled my mind much of the time. I left work at midnight, as usual, and stared at the clock in my car as I drove home, listening to the radio. It got to be 12:25 a.m., and the news came on.

At once, I thought that this request would not happen and how absurd it was even to think that it would. The news finished at 12:29, the D.J. talked a little, and at exactly 12:30 a.m., "Keeper of the Stars" began playing! It's a miracle that I didn't drive off the road. I screamed and cried, and my arms went wild. I sang the song as loud as my vocal cords could sing. As soon as I calmed down a little, I thanked my unseen friends profusely. I could actually hear them all laughing. A man's voice finally said, "How do you like that one!" My unseen friends laughed harder, and I screamed and cried again. Love totally filled me up. Tears streamed down my cheeks. My smile was so wide, my face hurt. It was real! I wasn't crazy!

#8

Power of Prayer

While growing up, I attended Catholic elementary school. Each day, we prayed for a long list of things and people. There were always special intentions for the saints and angels to do, and especially praying for those who had died and their suffering families. One day, I wondered about people who had died long ago who had no family. So that night, my prayers included unknown people from all over the world who had died, still needed prayers, but had no one left alive to pray for them.

Three or four years later, I saw for myself the power of prayer. It was in a dream-state experience that was as real as any experience of being awake. One of my guides was taking me somewhere, but we were flying. At times, we could see the Earth below. It was an incredible feeling of freedom and pure joy.

We were still flying, but I suddenly noticed we were about fifty feet above a large crowd of people. It was impossible to count how many there were. They all looked up at us, smiled, cheered, waved, and kept saying, "Thank you!" We were over them for quite a while. It was a wondrous sight to see. I thought they knew the guide with me. It felt so heartwarming, even though I did not know who they were. We never stopped.

Later, I asked my guide, "Who were those people? Why were they so happy to see us? Why were they saying thank you? Do you know all those people?"

My guide looked at me, smiled, and said, "Do you remember when you started to pray for people who had died, but had no one to pray for them? Well, those are the people you have been praying for. They wanted to see you so they could thank you, tell you how much you have helped them, and what a difference you've made in the evolution of their souls."

"Oh, my goodness. Yes, I remember, but that was quite a while ago. This is hard to believe. I've never been so surprised or felt so blessed to be honored like that!" Even in the dream-state, I felt emotional and cried. My guide finally convinced me that it was true and said, "When we align our intentions with God and focus our prayers on helping others, miraculous things happen."

While waiting in my chiropractor's office several years ago, I saw this quote. It expresses the awe-inspiring lesson I learned from this experience. I also mentioned it earlier in Part One.

"We never know how far-reaching something we may Think, Say, or Do Today...will affect the lives of millions tomorrow."

BY B. J. PALMER, D.C. PH.C.

#9

Explanation of Oneness

One concept we discussed during the intervention was "Oneness". My guide explained that all people and living things are connected, all are children of the Divine Force of God, and all are equal in the eyes of the Divine. I believed him, but couldn't understand how it was possible. My guide talked about reincarnation, the evolution of our souls, and how we contribute to the evolution of humanity each time we return to learn new, but different, life lessons. Over the years, I read lots of books and learned about reincarnation. However, the concept of "Oneness" and the fact that the evolution of our souls contributed to humanity as a whole baffled me. I struggled to understand it. Once again, I wondered about it all day. That night, I received a vision that explained the concept of "Oneness". It was one of the most profound visions I've had.

That night, I was approaching sleep still in that in-between state of mind. I was very relaxed, but not quite asleep. A vision appeared as if in a dream, but felt more realistic than a dream. In the vision, it was a very early summer day. I was all alone, standing at the edge of an ocean on a sandy beach. I was barefoot, wearing summer shorts and a T-shirt, because the temperature was comfortably warm. As far as I could see, the beach with pure white sand extended in both directions. The glow of the impending sunrise lit up the clear blue sky with a beautiful pink hue.

The water was calm, reflecting the colors of the sky with a hint of the sunrise. I listened to the gentle back-and-forth movement of the waves, which invited me in. I slowly started wading in. The water was surprisingly warm, and I continued farther out. By the time the water was just over my knees, the Sun became visible in the sky. Mesmerized, I stood there and watched the Sun come up over the horizon.

When the Sun was entirely above the water, I could look straight at it. It surprised me to realize the light of the Sun did not hurt my eyes! I could see all around the Sun with no difficulty. Then, utterly shocked and speechless, I observed the Sun being held in the palm of a huge hand! I kept thinking, "Oh my goodness. This must be the Hand of God!" I stood silently frozen, standing in the ocean water, watching this astonishing sight in awe.

Flames shot out from the Sun's surface. The larger flames of various sizes hung out there for a long period of time. The shorter flames of various sizes hung out for a short amount of time. Eventually, each flame fell back into the Sun and new flames emerged. Moments later, I saw images within each flame. The smaller flames were individual people. Some flames were even the lives of animals. Each of the larger flames included the lives of many people within a specific culture. There were millions of flames that were happening in all directions all over the Sun. I saw men, women, and children, who were Native Americans, Americans, Chinese, Europeans, Middle Easterners, Russians, and other cultures. The people included all colors, religions, and traditions. I also saw buffalos, elephants, whales, dolphins, eagles, and many more animals. All were continually moving and changing within each flame before falling back into the Sun, like they had probably done for eons of time. While watching this in awe, I realized we are being held and supported by the Hand of God. "WOW!" was my only thought, over and over.

After watching this for a while, I wondered what it all meant. I never heard words, but did receive a download explaining what was happening. I only hope I can accurately relay the significance of the symbolism of this vision.

Compared to eternity, the lifetime of an individual is very short. Human cultures last much longer and change a little with each new generation. We are aware of cultures that have disappeared. Other cultures develop. The individual flames coming from the Sun signify the lifetime of a person, a culture, an animal, and all life forms on Earth. We live our lives learning lessons to make life better for ourselves, our children, and generations to come. Even animals learn to adapt to changing conditions and teach their young what they learned. There is a continual evolution of learning and adaptation within each lifetime and within each culture.

The Sun symbolizes the whole of humanity and all other life forms on Earth. When a person is born, he or she leaves the whole of humanity, and appears as a flame, a lifetime. He or she lives a life learning lessons, gaining knowledge, understanding, and much wisdom to evolve his or her soul. As each person passes from life to death, the individual flame and all the knowledge that he or she learned along with the wisdom, falls back into the Sun, and returns to the whole. The updated knowledge, understanding, and wisdom are combined with everyone else's updated knowledge and experiences. As a result, each person contributes to and benefits from the evolution of the whole.

The flames appear for a time and then fall back into the whole of humanity, the body of the Sun - over and over again, only to reemerge as new flames with renewed wisdom continually evolving. Each new life, generation, or culture then appears from the whole as another flame with the benefit of the updated knowledge, understanding, and wisdom of all who have previously lived and learned and contributed to this evolution.

The multitude of people, animals, and cultures contributing to the evolution of knowledge are illustrated by the sizes of the flames and how long they stay as flames before falling back into the Sun. The body of the Sun illustrates the whole of humanity, and is how we are all interconnected, all sharing information and experiences, each gaining knowledge, understanding, and wisdom from those who lived before.

I thought about this for a while and think it could be the reason we see the actions of different people, animals, and cultures all over the world having similarities, even though they have no contact with or knowledge of the others.

This vision was my "ah-ha!" moment. The vision explained the concept of Oneness in a way I understood. After each lifetime, we contribute our experiences, good or bad, and knowledge from lessons learned to help future generations progress. We work with one another, respect each other, have integrity, be kind and caring, and love one another. What affects the whole ultimately affects the individual in future lifetimes.

The saying, 'What goes around, comes around,' gave me an entirely new understanding. We may never see what comes around, but we can be assured that it happens. There will always be shifting and changing, sometimes appearing as chaos, until all returns to balance and harmony within the whole of humanity!

It is heartwarming to notice that many young people of each new generation seem to have a higher level of conscious awareness of spirituality, responsibility, equality, and technology. They can adapt easier, quicker, and have a greater understanding of environmental concerns. I also believe that more of the young people from each new generation show more kindness, consideration, and love for all life, especially Mother Earth. They also seem to be observing life from a higher perspective with an open heart and soul while seeking truth, integrity, and equality for all.

In my humble opinion, this is the evolution of Oneness.

#10

My Brother's Transition

In June 1998, I experienced my second most profound spiritual experience of my life. It occurred at the time of my brother's transition to the Other Side. I was with him at his side before, during, and after his transition observing and feeling many emotions.

A year after high school graduation, my brother, John, was drafted into the Army. The Vietnam War was raging, and everyone was concerned. John reported for duty and finished boot camp in the Carolinas. He came home on a short leave before reporting for active duty on his return. His orders were to go to the Mekong Delta in Vietnam, where the fighting was at its peak. No one ever said it out loud, but everyone felt that when he left to report for duty, it would be the last time we would see him alive. The night before he was to leave, he and his buddies went out to party and to have a good time.

Later that night, there was a major car accident. John was a passenger in the front seat and was thrown forward, his head going through the windshield. There was a second car of friends who saw what happened and quickly went to help. The passenger door was open. John was unconscious, laying half in and half out of the car, bleeding profusely from his head. Fearing that the car might catch on fire, they pulled him out, laid him on the ground, and called for help. The ambulance came, loaded him in, and headed for the hospital's emergency room. My parents were notified and we quickly arrived at the ER. John received over 100 stitches in his head, but had no broken bones.

Everyone found it amazing. The doctor slapped him on his legs, telling him he would be okay. We were all relieved. Then John asked the doctor to slap him on the legs again. The doctor laughed, but did it anyway. Then, sounding like he was in shock, John told the doctor he did not feel his legs!

Everything changed in an instant. They transferred him to a larger hospital, and was in surgery within hours. Long story short - the accident paralyzed him from the neck down. For the next thirty years, he could move his arms a little, but not his hands or legs.

I could write a book about the trials and tribulations that he faced, plus the triumphs and accomplishments that he enjoyed during those thirty years. Everyone loved him for his love of life, sense of humor, and optimistic outlook - once he accepted his fate and no longer blamed God for his misfortune. He said more than once that "at least I didn't die in Vietnam or in that car accident."

Twenty-six years later, he was in the hospital on and off for the last four years of his life. Due to his paralysis, there was one complication after another. His body was shutting down, and there was nothing they could do for him.

John accepted the inevitable and was ready to say goodbye. Before he left the hospital, many of the doctors and nurses came to see him to say goodbye. They all agreed and told him he looked better than he had for weeks. John secretly told me he had seen our deceased father three times, and was ready to go with him the next time he saw him again. He was discharged from the hospital to be under the care of Hospice care and an ambulance brought John home for the last time.

Hospice came and instructed us what to do and what to expect. John did not want them to stay with him or have any of his close friends there, either. He had said his goodbyes to his friends in the hospital. John had tried to stay strong for them in the past, but felt he wasn't able to do that this time. He wanted each of them to remember the good times and not see him in that condition, since he wasn't sure what would happen. I and a close female friend of John's, along with my significant other, Bob, who was a Shaman, took care of John's needs and stayed with him.

John rested comfortably and slept until midnight. He woke up for about a half-hour and talked about his last wishes and whatever else was on his mind. He knew of some of my spiritual experiences, but did not know the extent of them. We had talked about them on and off during the past thirty years. He believed what I told him and thought it all sounded beautiful, but he had no personal experiences.

John fell back asleep. His female friend held his left hand, and I held his right hand. We sat there quietly for at least an hour, both in meditation and praying. John always slept with a towel over his head to block out any light in the room, and this time was no different.

Suddenly, his arms started moving around, obviously trying to get the towel off his head. He said nothing. I removed the towel. His face was looking up staring at the ceiling with his eyes wide open. I talked to him but got no response. I waved my hand in front of his eyes several times. He never blinked, and again, no response. I went back into meditation but wanted to speak to him. Knowing he might hear me at some level of consciousness, I asked my first question out loud: "Can you see the Light?"

Much to my shock and surprise, he moaned, "Ah huhhh."

His friend and I looked at each other in amazement, but we said nothing.

I continued, "Isn't the Light beautiful?"

He responded with another, "Ah huhhh."

"Are you okay?" There was no response.

"Can you feel the Love?"

He responded again, "Ah huhhh."

"Isn't it wonderful?" He then loudly moaned, "MMMMMMMMMMM."

With every question about the Light or Love or asking him about what he was seeing or feeling, we heard the same response. His wide eyes never stopped looking at the ceiling. I never saw him blink. He seemed to be in a blissful trance and never regained consciousness.

The questions with similar answers went on and off for several hours. We were relieved that he appeared to be in a euphoric state of bliss. We kept telling him that it was okay to leave us, that we would be alright, to take his time, and leave when it felt right for him to go.

During the Divine Intervention, my guide had explained that our souls and our bodies are independent of each other. I believed him, of course, and also read many books about it. Different religions had different philosophies. I believed my guide and never gave it another thought - until that night.

It was almost 4 a.m. and we had been quiet for a while. We were back in meditation when I saw something move in my mind's eye. My brother was still in bed, and we were still holding his hands. However, I could see his soul leave his physical body and start to walk away! This vision was shocking, surprising, and amazing all at the same time. Nothing like this had ever happened to me before. He was still breathing and his heart was still beating.

As I watched him slowly walk away, John paused and looked back at us. He stopped for a minute and smiled the biggest smile I'd seen him smile for a very long time. He started walking away again. In the distance, I could also see a small group of etheric White Light Beings waiting for him. They were tall and mostly translucent, but solid enough to know they were Heavenly Beings and possibly angels.

John stopped again and looked back, still looking so happy. He turned and walked to the group waiting for him. My brother was about six feet tall, and the Beings were twice that size. They gathered around him in a circle, and all walked off together! I watched until everyone disappeared.

His female friend, still holding his left hand, saw the same thing happen. We looked at each other, both on a spiritual high. "He did it. He made it. Wasn't that beautiful?!" That's all we kept saying. Words could not express how blessed we felt and how happy and grateful we were. We had received an unforgettable honor and privilege allowing us to see this sacred transition from physical life to the Spirit Realm! We still felt the pure Divine Unconditional Love filling our hearts and permeated everywhere.

Bob, John's friend, and I had been awake for about 36 hours. John's physical body was still breathing, and the heart was still beating. We knew that John was not there. He had left. During my Divine Intervention, my guide had told me about the body and the soul being separate. This experience definitely confirmed that for me!

Bob was holding sacred space in the house all night, keeping the energies high, not allowing anything negative to enter. We told him what happened. We were all thrilled that the transition had occurred with love, ease, and grace. I wanted to rest a bit while Bob continued to watch the energy of the space.

About an hour later, Bob woke me up and told me that John and my deceased father had just visited the house. They were both on what looked like a magic carpet flying around the inside of the house. My father was sitting up front in control, with my brother behind him. Their visit lasted less than one minute, and then they flew through the bedroom wall and disappeared!

Bob wanted us to check John's breathing and pulse. He was convinced that neither would be present, and he was correct. The time was between 5 and 6 a.m. It was done - less than 24 hours after being discharged from the hospital. It all seemed bittersweet. We were happy and excited for John, now free of so many limitations and hardships. We were left with our loving memories, but an emptiness in our hearts.

After resting a few days, my memories still kept taking me back to that night for many reasons, and would continue to do so for years to come. Seeing John walk away with that big smile was wonderful, since I hadn't seen him walk for thirty years. It didn't matter that it was his soul walking away. He was free of his paralyzed physical body.

It was how he walked away and looked back at us that reminded me of the 1990 movie "Ghost," with Patrick Swayze and Demi Moore. Patrick Swayze said his last goodbyes, looked back at Demi Moore a couple of times, and then walked into the bright White Light in front of him and disappeared. It took quite a while before I could rent that movie and watch it again. When I did, I was right. The ending of the movie was similar. I felt like I relived that night all over again. It was beautiful beyond words, and, of course, I cried and cried.

Very few people have heard this story, but I now feel that it should be told. My Divine Intervention dissolved my fear of death long ago. This privileged observation was another confirmation for me that there is nothing to fear when making our transition. There is no real death - only a different form of life.

#11

Second Dream Experience

One day in 2003, I was deep in thought about my intervention dream, which took place in the late 1960s. I was thinking about the spiritual aspects of life and what it's like on the Other Side. Since the intervention, I've received multiple visions and spiritual insights over the past thirty years. It was possible to ask a question and usually receive a mental download of information or a vision explaining an entire concept. So, I asked what should I do with all this valuable information? In my heart, I believed these spiritual insights could help each person have a much happier and more fulfilled life.

Four or five nights later, I was almost ready to give up on receiving a message. Fortunately, I had another even more powerful, beautiful, and amazing dream experience! I call it a dream only because it occurred in the dream-state, but it felt as real as if I was actually there on the Other Side - and there for a long time.

This time, my guide was a different guide and teacher, but looked very much like an older Jacob from years before. I smiled and Jacob must have read my mind. He also smiled and said, "Yes, you are correct. We can appear to people in any form or age that will produce comfort without fear. It is nice to see you again. I am pleased that you changed your path there on Earth. Shall we continue with more extensive lessons this time?"

I was brimming over with joy and quickly responded, "Yes, of course. I've been waiting many years to see and speak with you again. The earlier insights during that one night gave me so much hope for my future, along with faith and trust in the Divine. It changed my life. The revelations of that night were a quick overview, but still enough to help me see things from God's expansive perspective instead of my limited narrow-focused thoughts, beliefs, opinions, and perspectives. For that, I will be forever grateful!"

Jacob then talked about and gave examples of how important it is to obtain a knowledge of all aspects of life to increase our understanding of life, death, and the afterlife. This knowledge would increase our wisdom more than you can imagine. Our thoughts and beliefs would change, along with our outlook on life. Decisions would be made easier. Outcomes would be more aligned with our happiness. Relationships and perspectives would be expanded. Our lives would be happier, more fulfilled, and more purposeful. Our dreams and desires would come true.

He also said that there was much to learn about the connections of our physical, mental, emotional, and spiritual energies within the Physical and the Spirit Realms through the Divine soul within each of us. In the course of this seemingly very long dream, Jacob told me that I would also meet five other teachers/guides.

Jacob was the first and last teacher/guide in this dream experience, with the other five appearing in between. Each one shared knowledge about different aspects of life in both the Physical and Spirit Realms. Each one gave excellent examples with explanations. All the information confirmed and added much to the information provided to me in my first life-changing intervention dream experience.

The following are the teachers/guides that discussed different aspects of life and death. The actual discussions are in Part One of the book: See the Table of Contents.

Jacob - the energies of the physical body, life, and transformation.

Robert - the first level in the Spirit Realm and our soul energy.

Rebecca - the transformation of water comparing different states of being.

Matthew - the Spirit Realm, our soul energy in the Physical and Spirit Realms.

Benjamin - Nature and how plant life parallels human life.

Francis - Nature and compared animal instinct with human intuition.

Jacob - concluded with Universal Forces of God and the purpose of life and our soul.

All this information seemed to be important wisdom to me, and I thought it could possibly help other people on their journey of life. I asked my guides again what should I do about this? "Write a book" is what I heard. I panicked and thought I would need to find someone to do that. I asked again, and my guides told me that the book was mine to write. It terrified me because I had no experience writing anything, but somehow knew I would eventually do my best and write it.

So now, many years later, I still feel this information is important to help answer mystical questions that others may have. This book combines the information revealed to me in both the original and second dream experiences provided by six teachers/guides in seven sessions. This is my true story, and am aware that experiences and beliefs vary with each person. So, as always, keep what resonates at the moment and leave the rest. Life is an incredible adventure to be embraced and enjoyed, no matter what!

#12

Cosmic Consciousness ~ 2008

The stars, the moon, the solar system, and the galaxy have always mesmerized me. Looking for constellations and finding the brightest stars was fun and exciting. Whenever there was a lightning storm, I was perched in my favorite place to be, the window of our enclosed sun porch. Close lightning strikes would light up the sky in amazingly beautiful streaks of light. It gave me great pleasure to watch this phenomenon.

When the television series "Star Trek" began, it became my must-see program every week. The same became true of the series "Stargate." It all seemed real to me and possibly true on some level of awareness. I convinced myself that both television shows contained an insight into consciousness beyond normal daily living. There were also several dream experiences that convinced me of life out in the galaxy and the Universe. My belief is we are not alone and have never been alone.

In 2008, a good friend of mine asked if I wanted to go to Asheville, North Carolina, to see Dr. Steven Greer. I had never heard of him before. She explained he used to be an emergency room doctor in Asheville. Now his mission was to contact friendly extraterrestrial beings, ETs, from other planetary star systems. These benevolent beings exist in higher dimensions and are spiritually evolved with a higher level of consciousness, similar to that of Christ Consciousness. They are here to help serve the greater good for all beings.

Years before, Dr. Greer had compiled multiple reports with evidence of ETs. The reports mentioned that the government had these records, but would not disclose them to the public. Dr. Greer was taking on the task of disclosing the facts to the people. He was training anyone interested in contacting these benevolent high-vibrational ETs and possibly having a personal experience. This trip definitely intrigued me, and I said yes to going with my friend to Ashville.

We spent a Friday evening listening to a lecture by Dr. Greer. He explained the history of his endeavors and the massive amount of information he had acquired. Saturday was an all-day workshop learning about Dr. Greer's protocols for making contact and what to expect once contact was made. Saturday night, we went to a remote area in the country to a large, cleared field.

Our group of about forty people formed a large circle, while Dr. Greer and his crew set up equipment to send and receive electromagnetic signals. We went into meditation because contact is usually made with telepathy. It seemed as though we were in meditation for a short time, but at least an hour had passed. When we returned to the conscious state, people shared their experiences. Most of the people made contact. Some people saw and experienced the same thing. Most people had individual experiences. Some were healed, some heard messages, and some saw and talked to Beings within a spaceship unseen by our three-dimensional vision.

My personal experience, while in meditation, was seeing the outside of a massive spaceship from below. It was so large that I couldn't see the outer edges. The next thing I knew, I was inside this spaceship, standing at a window looking outside. The scenery was the same as when I was on the ground, but I was looking down from a much higher viewpoint. I saw no beings nor received any messages.

I believed the spaceship was directly above the field in which we had gathered before meditation. It was an experience I don't think I'll ever forget. There was no fear or panic from anyone. All messages were positive, helpful, and enlightening. One message was to teach this protocol to others. Another message was that they wish to help humanity. I said nothing when others were sharing experiences. Later, Dr. Greer electronically confirmed a large spaceship had been directly above the center of the field we were in. It was my confirmation, and I later wrote to him about my experience.

My friend and I talked about this for hours on the way back home. I felt bad because I had no one to talk to about this, let alone teach it to. Almost a year later, I was listening to a radio program on the internet. Two women were being interviewed who Dr. Greer had also trained. They had formed a close encounter of the 5th kind, CE-5, group in upstate New York. Thanks to the internet, I found the phone number for one of the women and called her. Soon after that, several of my friends and I joined her group.

The first time we attended, everyone clearly saw a small UFO ship. It was about 1,500 feet above us for at least ten seconds as it flew over the group! There was no sound whatsoever. It was late evening, but we still had enough light to see it clearly. Even though I had a camera with me, I never took a picture. My eyes were glued to the visible UFO. We attended monthly group meetings and often saw the presence of many UFOs. They were much higher in the sky, though. Once it was dark, we watched the changing brightness of light emitted from each UFO, along with the speed and drastic sudden changes of direction of single and/or groups of them. Some people in the group perceived Beings on the ground, but that was never my experience.

Since then, I have been in several groups that have watched the skies, made contact, and received messages with telepathy. Several people in each group received messages. The most common were: they come in peace; they are here to help expand our consciousness; to help us gain clarity about our spiritual path in life; and, especially, to aid in humanity's spiritual maturity. I have learned much over the years, but I believe there's a lot more to come.

#13

Discovery of the Violet Flame

One beautiful day in early May 2011, they blessed me with a day off from work. The week had been long, with lots of overtime. Mowing the lawn or any physical exercise always helped me relax and reduce stress. It was a warm, dry day with a cloudless blue sky. After a couple of hours of using the manual push mower, a long-needed break was necessary. While relaxing on my covered porch, a refreshing breeze cooled me off. As I sat there enjoying the peace and quiet, I was mesmerized by the beauty of the woods close to the house.

Suddenly, from the direction of the woods, I saw an etheric vision of a small face quickly zooming toward me, getting larger as the vision came closer. I was wide awake but could see this translucent vision of a beautiful woman's face, with striking features, appearing right in front of my face. Nothing like that had ever happened before. I looked at her for a few seconds, before her face quickly zoomed back out and disappeared! Nothing was spoken, and I heard no telepathic message.

After the woman's face disappeared, almost at once, another similar vision zoomed toward me. This time, it was an etheric vision of the face of a man. The same thing happened. His small translucent face zoomed in toward my face, also getting larger as the vision came closer, stopping right in front of my face. For a few seconds, I gazed into his radiantly beautiful face before his face also zoomed back out, getting smaller and smaller as it also disappeared!

I was stunned and in awe of this experience, and continued staring in the same direction. As soon as the man's face disappeared, a third vision surprisingly appeared. It was similar to the other two, but was different. As the translucent vision came closer, it looked like the flame of a candle, but there was no candle - just a flame all by itself. The color of the outside of the flame was deep purple, the middle was a rich yellow color, and the center was bright white. I had seen nothing like that either. The flame was also in front of my face for a few seconds before it quickly zoomed back out and disappeared!

"WOW!" was all I could say to myself. I sat on the porch in awe for a long time that day. I instantly knew that there was great meaning in these visions, but no idea what it could be. I had recently met a woman at a local Spiritual Arts Fair who lived outside of Syracuse, NY. She was spiritually gifted with abilities to channel and give readings for people and their pets. I thought she probably could explain what I had seen, so I called her. Once I explained what had happened, she quickly told me that I had seen Mother Mary, Saint Germaine, and the Violet Flame. The Violet Flame was completely new to me. My new friend explained a little about it.

By the end of that week, another miracle occurred. I received an unsolicited letter from Patricia Cotta-Robles of Arizona. I had never heard of her before. The letter explained many things about the power of the Violet Flame. I was shocked and completely flabbergasted. These visions seemed like a miracle. I was astonished that I received powerful information in the mail about the Violet Flame. Eventually, I realized the visions were real.

The Violet Flame is of Divine Love, and considered the sacred fire of the Holy Spirit. It is a high frequency Light that can be used to change your life. This Violet Flame, also called the Violet Fire, dissolves negative energy and transmutes/restores it into positive energy. For thousands of years, it was a secret, known only by spiritual leaders and experienced by mystics. Today, it is associated with Saint Germain.

This experience and learning about the Violet Flame has blessed me in many ways. It has helped me make many necessary changes in my life. Now, I get to collaborate with the Divine every day, and still think about that memorable day often.

#14

Star Blessings

The gifted woman I met at the local Spiritual Arts Fair, which I told you about in the last story, also conducted Star Blessing ceremonies for individuals with open hearts and souls. Each person would expand his or her conscious awareness and have a deeper connection with the cosmos and the Divine. We would expand to receive messages from star beings, Ascended Masters, Archangels, or other Divine beings with Christ Consciousness, each a messenger of God.

Out of curiosity, one of my friends and I traveled to Syracuse, NY, for the first of twelve possible Star Blessing meetings and ceremonies. We were pleasantly surprised by the results of the first ceremony. It was at this meeting that St. Germain first came to me and channeled messages. It was an amazing experience to hear him as my thoughts, realizing that it was St. Germain speaking to me. I am blessed to still be channeling him at this time, and sometimes other Divine Beings.

In past times, I knew I received channeled messages from high vibrational beings, but not sure if they were from St. Germain, the angels, my Higher Self, God, or some other spiritual being. Gratitude filled me every time a question was answered, a request was fulfilled, and help was given when asked for.

Each month, there was another Star Blessing to open and expand conscious awareness to more of the unseen realities of the Divine Spirit Realm. There were twelve in all, but we only attended three of them. Each session was an enlightening experience, but circumstances changed, and neither of us could continue.

#15

Death of Family

One by one, my family members passed from the physical world to the Spirit Realm. My mother was the first to leave. She suffered one serious health condition after another. Though she was strong for years, she never accepted the reality of my brother's car accident and his paralysis. After the car accident, her health continued to decline. Eighteen years later, she was dealing with diabetes, breast cancer, arthritis, a couple of heart attacks, and finally, congestive heart failure. One last massive heart attack freed her from her pain.

My father was next to leave, fourteen years later. When my mother died, he retired after working hard all his life. He also had two or three heart attacks, which eventually turned into congestive heart failure. He was strong for a long time, but he too was never the same after my brother's accident. Toward the end of his life, Hospice helped keep him comfortable, and he lived twice as long as expected.

There is one memory that has stayed with me for all these years. My father had an oxygen machine and slept most of the time. Hospice volunteers or I would take turns sitting with him in case he woke up and needed something. It was my turn, and I sat next to his bed, quietly reading a book. I saw him move, and looked up from the book. His eyes were closed. He slowly sat straight up with his right hand extended out in front of him, as if to grab hold of something. Suddenly, he jerked a little and looked right at me. Calmly, I asked him where he was going. Just as calmly, he said he was going to the woods to hunt with his father. It suddenly dawned on him what he told me, that he had seen his deceased father, and was about to join him. My father laughed a little, before lying back down and falling right back to sleep.

Once again, I had received confirmation about life on the Other Side. It was a beautiful moment. I was happy that my grandpa was there for my father that day, and would be again to help him make the transition, which was soon after this experience.

After seven more years, in 1998, my only sibling followed. My brother, John, was a year older than me, minus four days. We always laughed about being the same age for those four days. For thirty years after his car accident, he endured his paralysis and, at times, also enjoyed his life greatly. His transition was within 24 hours of obtaining help from Hospice. At his bedside in meditation, I witnessed his transition, truly a blessing beyond words. See story #10 for the entire amazing experience.

In 2011, the last person in my earthly family to leave this physical life was my partner, Bob, in 2011. Many years had passed since our first date. We saw each other almost every day after that. He was not well for almost ten years. After smoking most of his life, he struggled with COPD and coronary artery disease.

He was the most stubborn man I had ever met, not wanting or accepting help from anyone other than me. He even refused to go to a doctor or allow Hospice to come in. The morning that he died, I was scheduled to work. Before I left, I found him slumped over, his face with a purple hue, and not breathing. At once, I called 911. The ambulance crew came right away, but it was too late. Even though I knew it was inevitable, it was still traumatic. Because it was an unattended death and without a medical directive, the coroner and the N.Y.S. troopers both needed to investigate, which was also traumatic.

Soon after the 911 call, I received another confirmation of unseen help from above. Friends who lived fifteen minutes away owned a scanner to hear all the fire and ambulance calls, but it had not worked for quite a while. They planned on replacing it, but never did. Early that morning, while getting ready to go away for the weekend, the scanner went off. Shocked to hear it blare into life, they went to listen. The scanner call turned out to be my 911 call! It gave enough information that they knew the 911 call was from our house. The wife called me right away. They both came to the house just after the troopers arrived. I was blessed and grateful to have those friends rush over and stay with me until the ambulance crew took Bob's body to the hospital. I was also grateful to have another good friend work for me the entire weekend.

When I calmed down, but was still upset, I was relieved for Bob. I knew he would finally be without pain and no longer struggle for every breath. He was free at last. The rest of my day was spent outside, alone on the covered porch surrounded by Nature.

Everyone had left the house. It was late afternoon and still a beautiful, warm July day. I was still sitting on the covered porch, staring into space. There was a folding lawn chair opposite mine. I noticed that a chickadee, one of my totem birds, had landed on the front edge of the chair. It stared right at me! No bird had ever done that to me before. I stared back at the bird. It cocked its little head left and right a couple of times and even chirped as if it were talking to me. The chickadee flapped its wings several times, looked straight at me again for a few moments, and then flew off.

Somehow, I felt that this bird was telling me that my partner Bob was fine and free as a bird. I cried again and went into the house to get more tissues. The radio was on a country station, because Bob loved Willie Nelson and the older country music. I usually had the radio on since I love music of any kind. It usually helps to lift my spirits and soothes my soul. Within a minute of being inside, I was stunned to hear a Willie Nelson song play. It stopped me in my tracks. The song was "Blue Skies!" I was surprised and unaware that Willie Nelson had ever recorded that song, since I had never heard him sing it before. I paid attention to the lyrics for the first time. It was as if Bob was talking to me again. The song was another wonderful confirmation for me that he was okay and how beautiful it is on the Other Side. My heart soared, and I cried once again, but with tears of joy. I knew for sure that he was in the Spirit Realm safe and sound.

#16

Energy Healing

All my life, my full-time job had been working in several hospital laboratories around New York State. My second full-time job was taking care of family members with serious medical conditions one-by-one, for many years. During my Divine Intervention, my guide told me I had many people to take care of in my life. It seemed natural that they would include my family. After each one transitioned, I was happy they were free of the trials and tribulations of life. But now, I was feeling alone and lost, not sure of what I wanted to do, not sure of anything. It felt like the dark night of the soul.

For about six months, I continued to work full time, just going through the motions. I lost myself somewhere along the way, putting everyone else's needs as the priority. But now I was alone and on my own. There was no one left who I needed to take care of except myself. It was a surreal feeling and realized that I had lots of inner work to do. I wasn't sure what I liked and disliked, what I wanted to do for fun, what foods I preferred, where I would like to visit, or what was the priority of my life in the future. It was the beginning of a glorious adventure!

Eventually, I could think about other things, especially spiritual experiences, which lifted my spirits, gave me hope, and restored my soul. Energy healing had always been a significant interest of mine. Throughout the years, I read many books to understand the principles and techniques of several healing modalities. My family members had volunteered to let me practice on them as

I learned the techniques of each modality. They were happy to reap the rewards of feeling better each time.

It finally dawned on me. I had the freedom to pursue formal training to learn how to balance and harmonize the energies of other people. That's what I did. I enjoyed meeting many kind and talented people in the world of energy healing. Each type, or modality, works a little differently. During the process, God, personal guides, angels, ascended masters, and/or multidimensional beings are called on for aid. Each modality sends higher vibrational frequencies, in their own way, to help relax, clean, clear, and transmute discordant energies in and around the client's body. These vibrational frequencies flood the body and the surrounding energy field with love. It's like realigning and rebooting the energetic system of a computer, but it is the energetic system of the physical body. These energies are spiritually guided to the areas of greatest need, physical, mental, emotional, or spiritual, for the client's greatest well-being.

By being a conduit for the unseen Universal Forces of Divine Love, I once again remembered and felt the incredible emotion of Unconditional Love I experienced during my intervention. It gives me great pleasure to say I am an energy healing practitioner and is still an important part of my life.

#17

Hermetic Principles

This experience occurred one night, years ago, during the time of my Solar Return. The Solar Return is the exact astrological positioning of the planets on the day and time of your birth. There is a slight difference each year, but the exact time can be calculated. Many people believe the influence of the planets helps fulfill wishes and dreams for the coming year. People also believe the influence varies five hours before and five hours after the exact solar return time. Some consider this ten-hour period of time as ten hours of power to express intentions for the coming year, and receive help to accomplish those intentions throughout the year from the unseen forces of the Universe.

I had written a list of intentions and things to do during my ten hours of power to reflect the list of accomplishments I desired in the coming year. The exact solar return time was approaching, and I needed to go outdoors in the dark, build a fire, and read my list. It was cloudy and I could not see any stars. It was January in the northeast, after midnight, and very cold. The fire was warm and bright as I invited all of my guides, teachers, and everyone else aligned with my mission and purpose for the coming year to witness the reading of my intentions. I read all of them out loud and then burned the list in the fire, releasing my intentions to the Universe to help fulfill my plans.

When finished, I sat down to enjoy the warmth of the fire. I looked up at the sky, thinking about all my invisible friends that were invited. I almost fell over! The sky was clear and cloudless, with many bright stars. It made me dizzy and took my breath away. I couldn't believe that the sky had dramatically changed in such a short time. Smiling from ear to ear, I thanked each of my unseen friends. I knew they had heard me. When the fire was almost out and I could leave it, I went back inside the house.

Channeling was the only thing left that I wanted to do during the solar return timing. Usually, St. Germain comes through, but the energy and words were different. Earlier in the month, I read a channeled message from a multi-dimensional Being on the Starship Bethlehem. After channeling for a short time, it sounded familiar, and I asked who was speaking to me.

It was the same Being from the Starship! One of the things he told me was - "If I really meant what I intended for the coming year, I should teach the way of "The Kybalion!" I did not know what "The Kybalion" was, although it was an amazing suggestion, and I was interested in finding out. The message confirmed for me that my invisible friends were listening and were starting to help right away.

The next morning, I googled "The Kybalion" and printed it out. It turned out to be the Hermetic Principles. These principles are word-of-mouth teachings taught in the mystery schools for thousands of years. This book was the first time initiates had written it down for all to learn. The Yogi Society published it in Chicago in 1908. The Kybalion is available on the internet, and can be printed out free to read and study if interested.

It took at least a year to study and learn from it before I felt comfortable sharing it in classes. Although it included all kingdoms, I concentrated on humanity only and how each of the principles related to humankind. This information and wisdom are still relevant today in modern times. I have continued to share this timeless wisdom, and how we can still apply these principles today. In my humble opinion, this information represents the Universal Laws, Cosmic Laws, and Laws of Nature on all levels.

In 2018, I met a woman in southern France who was currently at the eleventh of twelve levels of an Egyptian Mystery School. She talked about the Hermetic Principles, and when asked, she confirmed that those principles were the basis of the teachings of the current mystery school. This coincidence once again confirmed for me that our unseen friends are listening and helping us every step of the way on our path, our journey of life.

~ *"...for those who have the eyes to see and the ears to hear..."* ~

#18

Locked in Bathroom

About ten years ago, I received a profound confirmation that our unseen friends are always ready to help. I can laugh about it now, but it was scary when it happened.

It was fall, and I was expecting another snowy, cold winter in the Northeast. The previous year had been terrible, with too much snow and frigid temperatures. I was still working in a local hospital lab, needing to leave my house in the country by 6:30 a.m. It was getting harder to wake up at 3:00 a.m. to clear snow and still get to work on time. I decided to move to the city for the winter and rent a house close to the hospital, so I could walk to work and avoid all the problems.

In late fall, I moved into a small but very nice older home. Early morning the next day, I was getting ready for work, which included taking a shower. I had pulled the bathroom door closed out of habit, even though no one else was in the house. When ready to leave the bathroom, to my shock and surprise, the door wouldn't open!

There was no lock on the door. I couldn't understand why or how this had happened. It was a solid wooden door with an older glass doorknob and an old-fashioned keyhole. No matter how I jiggled the knob, the door would not open. There were two screws holding the doorknob in place. I rummaged around the medicine cabinet and under the sink, looking for something to help take the screws out. I found a small pair of scissors and tried to loosen the screws. One came out, but the other would not budge.

By this time, 15 to 20 minutes had passed. I was starting to panic. No one at work knew where I had moved to. The property owner would have already gone to work. Then I realized that I didn't have my cell phone anyway.

There certainly wasn't a phone in the bathroom. Panic flooded over me! I was naked in the bathroom with only a towel around me and no means to contact anyone. No one knew where I was. Even if work called wondering why I was late, there would be no answer. There was nothing I could do about it. My panicked mind went right to the thought that I could die in here before anyone would find me!

Suddenly, I realized I needed to calm down and think. A few minutes later, I started to pray, talked to my guides, and asked for their help. They were my only hope of getting out of this bathroom. There was nothing more I could do about this situation. Remembering the experience of hearing the song 'Keeper of the Stars' being played at 12:30 a.m. years before, I knew my guides could do anything. I calmly sat on the top of the toilet seat and waited.

After 5 or 10 minutes, I distinctly heard a soft voice in my head clearly say, "Try the door again now." I got up and jiggled the doorknob for only five to ten seconds. The door opened! I screamed and cried with relief. My body was shaking inside and out, as if I was in shock. Without waiting another second, I left that bathroom as fast as my feet would take me. I sat down in the bedroom to breathe and calm down.

Eventually, I realized another miracle had happened! I thanked my guides profusely with Love, Gratitude, Appreciation, and Blessings beyond measure for hearing me, coming to my rescue, and being there to help me relax.

They even got me to work on time, which to me, was another miracle. I never closed that bathroom door again!

This quote became a literal confirmation for me, "Knock, and the door will open. Ask and you shall receive."

Our unseen angels, guides, and God are always there to help each of us just a thought away!"

We just have to remember to ask for their help!

ABOUT THE AUTHOR

Sharon Wagner is a teacher, channeler, and an energy healing practitioner. She helps people bring more balance and harmony into their physical, mental, emotional, and spiritual bodies for a more peaceful life. She has studied energy healing modalities, earning certifications as a Reiki Master, an Integrated Energy Therapy (I.E.T.) Master Instructor, and in Quantum Arcturian Energy Healing.

Sharon also pursued her love of science, earning an Associate of Applied Science (A.A.S.) degree in Medical Laboratory Technology and a Bachelor of Science (BS) degree in Math and Science. She obtained multiple medical laboratory certifications while working full-time in various hospital laboratories for over 40 years, with a concentration in Microbiology.

In 2021, Sharon retired and is now happily pursuing her spiritual dreams and desires.